T0295562

THE TOURIST EXPERIENCE

Series Editor: Richard Sharpley

The Tourist Experience series addresses a notable gap in the literature on Tourism Studies by foregrounding the tourist experience in a cohesive and thematically structured manner.

Taking a novel approach by presenting both short form publications and longer form monographs exploring issues in the tourist experience, the series will seek to build a comprehensive set of texts that collectively contribute to critical discourse and understanding of the contemporary tourist experience. Short form publications will review specific types of tourist by focusing primarily on the influences and nature and significance of their experiences within a socio-cultural framework while longer titles will embrace contemporary empirical and conceptual perspectives and debates as a means of understanding experiences.

The Creative Tourist

The Creative Tourist:
A Eudaimonic Perspective

BY

XAVIER MATTEUCCI
Independent Scholar, Austria

AND

MELANIE KAY SMITH
Budapest Metropolitan University, Hungary

United Kingdom – North America – Japan – India – Malaysia – China

Emerald Publishing Limited
Emerald Publishing, Floor 5, Northspring, 21-23 Wellington Street, Leeds LS1 4DL.

First edition 2024

British Library Cataloguing in Publication Data
A catalogue record for this book is available from the British Library

ISBN: 978-1-83753-405-0 (Print)
ISBN: 978-1-83753-404-3 (Online)
ISBN: 978-1-83753-406-7 (Epub)

INVESTOR IN PEOPLE

Contents

List of Figures and Tables

Figure

Tables

About the Authors

Dr Xavier Matteucci is an Independent Scholar currently employed at FHWien der WKW / University of Applied Sciences for Management and Communication. He was appointed Honorary Professor at IMC Krems University of Applied Sciences, Austria in 2023. He grew up in the Provence region where, over the years, he has witnessed the erosion of the regional culture and the marketisation and privatisation of public spaces and services. He became interested in the influence of tourism/travel on individual and collective well-being as well as in the effects of globalisation processes on regional cultures and cultural identities. During his frequent travel to Spain, he became passionate about flamenco as an art form, which led to his doctoral research on creative flamenco experiences. Xavier adheres to constructivist epistemology, but he also finds inspiration in new materialist philosophies for understanding social phenomena and fostering positive change. His publications cover topics in the areas of tourism experiences and well-being, cultural tourism and qualitative social research methodologies. Apart from his academic activities, he has led European Commission funded consultancy research projects on sustainable cultural tourism in South-East Europe.

Dr Melanie Kay Smith is an Associate Professor and Researcher in Urban Studies, Cultural Heritage, Well-being and Tourism. She currently works at Budapest Metropolitan University in Hungary and the University of Tartu Pärnu College in Estonia and is a PhD Supervisor at Corvinus University Budapest. She is also a Research Associate at the Department of Historical and Heritage Studies, Faculty of Humanities, University of Pretoria, South Africa. She has been an Academic and Researcher for over 20 years with lecturing and degree programme management experience in the UK, Hungary, Estonia, Austria, Germany and Switzerland. She has a PhD in Culture-led Urban Regeneration and Planning and over 100 publications including several books, book chapters and academic articles. She has been an invited Keynote Speaker at Conferences in more than 20 countries. She was Chair of ATLAS (Association for Tourism and Leisure Education and Research) for seven years (2005–2012) and has been an Expert Advisor or Consultant on projects in several countries, including UNWTO/ETC (2016–2018).

Acknowledgements

Many individuals have inspired us over the years. It is often difficult to name just a few because this book is the product of many years of reading exciting and provocative books and articles and of many encounters and discussions with inspiring friends, colleagues and other people we have met along the way. A large source of inspiration also comes from some creative tourists themselves for finding the strength to leave their comfort zone ansd venture into the world. In particular, XM is indebted to the creative flamenco tourists who enthusiastically embraced his scholarly endeavour and graciously shared their experiences. Some of their experiences are presented in this book. XM is also grateful to Ivana Volić for her generous support and patience throughout. Un grand MERCI à Albert, Lola, Léo et Lino. MS would like to thank Greg Richards for his inspiration over the years in the fields of both cultural and creative tourism. She is also grateful for the many wonderful shared cultural experiences and creative moments with her husband and sons, especially Levi, who is training to be a dancer. Lastly, we would like to thank Professor Richard Sharpley, as the book series editor and Nick Wallwork, senior commissioning editor at Emerald for their forbearance with this project.

Chapter 1

Introduction

Natalie, a 32-year-old Canadian woman from Alberta, has come to Spain to partake in flamenco dance classes. She wears flip-flops – the ubiquitous rubber beachwear – but her left foot is covered with band-aids. During the course of our conversation, Natalie provides a crisp summary of her creative tourist experience; she discloses that her experience has been

> Enlightening. Productive ... because it's not like it's been a regular vacation where you go just to see stuff, it's like I'm actually taking courses, I'm living it. Um ... Difficult [laugh] and occasionally painful [chuckles]. It's because my left foot hurts.

The words articulated by Natalie clearly reveal that her trip has not only been smooth and pleasurable as one may expect a summer holiday in Spain to be. Natalie's creative tourist experience in the cramped spaces of her flamenco dance school in Seville stands in sharp contrast to the daily white sandy *playa* experience of other tourists in Marbella or Tarifa. Learning, discovering, sharing, bonding, feeling, performing, resisting, creating, flourishing and becoming count among the key experiential modalities that punctuate the chapters of this book about the creative tourist. These experiential modalities set the tone for what lies beneath the surface of the creative tourist experience.

Much has been written about the nexus between creativity and tourism, yet little is known about the central protagonist in what is now commonly known as *creative tourism*. With this book, we therefore hope to offer a nuanced understanding of the creative tourist experience. Creative tourism can be linked to different activities and contexts. Furthermore, creative tourism has been narrowly and broadly defined based on different levels of tourist involvement within a variety of contexts (Duxbury & Richards, 2019; Richards, 2011). Here, we understand creative tourism as a subset of cultural tourism, whereby tourists interact with inspirational locals and engage with place-specific endogenous resources for self-fulfilment purposes. Our understanding of creative tourism, therefore, resonates with Richards and Raymond's (2000) early definition of this concept and

The Creative Tourist: A Eudaimonic Perspective, 1–15
Copyright © 2024 by Xavier Matteucci and Melanie Kay Smith
Published under exclusive licence by Emerald Publishing Limited
doi:10.1108/978-1-83753-404-320241001

with de Bruin and Jelinčić's (2016) notion of participatory experience tourism, which both emphasise learning and greater intensity of involvement. Likewise, we relate to the four dimensions of creative tourism, as suggested by Bakas, Duxbury and Castro (2018), which are: active participation, a learning process, opportunities for self-expression and community engagement. The United Nations Educational, Scientific and Cultural Organization (UNESCO) (2006) advocated that creative tourism should include more access to culture and history, authentic engagement in the real and unique cultural life of a place, as well as more interaction with living culture and the people who live there. The creative tourist, for example, might be blowing glass in the picturesque village of Biot in the Provence region, kneading sourdough bread in Saint-Jean-Port-Joli in the province of Québec or practicing flamenco in Seville, the bustling and colourful Andalusian capital. As Natalie's words above suggest, *doing* rather than *being there* lies at the core of creative tourism.

As a participatory form of cultural tourism, creative tourism is primarily based on the intangible heritage and the traditional practices of indigenous communities (Smith, 2016) and it is driven by the desire to learn, to share and to create. If creative tourists want to have fun like other tourists, they seem to be more concerned with authentic cultural encounters, self-exploration and the construction of their identities (Argod, 2014). In other words, creative tourists aspire to live their life well; this means living a meaningful life, or a life that reflects their core values. A life well-lived is what Greek philosopher Aristotle called *eudaimonia* in Nicomachean Ethics. Since the creative tourist is driven by a quest for meaning and a search for happiness (Matteucci, 2018), in this book, we portray the creative tourist experience as eudaimonic.

Why do we need a book on the creative tourist? Firstly, creative tourism has been presented as a more ethical and sustainable form of travel (e.g. Matteucci, Nawijn, & von Zumbusch, 2022; Scherf, 2021). Creative tourists tend to stay longer at the same destination than other tourists and because their consumption pattern resembles that of residents, the money spent by creative tourists contributes to the wider community. Richards (2021a) and Scherf (2021) note that resident-tourist relationships based on culture and creativity can enhance residents' quality of life and more generally improve the sustainability of destinations. In addition, because residents tend to be on an equal footing with tourists who seek out their creativity and expertise (Richards, 2021b), the tourist-host encounter is considered to be more egalitarian (Duxbury & Bakas, 2021). The creative tourist-host encounter is beneficial to both protagonists for a host of other reasons. For instance, their relational encounters foster local knowledge production (Braidotti, 2019), stimulate creativity (Bryden & Gezelius, 2017) and promote care and preservation of heritage as well as stewardship (Sterling, 2020). Benefits might also include cultural revival, reinforcing local pride and identity. In light of the many issues arising from overtourism, any tourism activity that has the potential to provide communities with significant benefits is worth some attention.

Secondly, creative tourism has been praised for its transformative potential. For instance, Duxbury and Bakas (2021) argue that creative tourism promotes human well-being, positive emotions, mindfulness and self-knowledge. Self-transformation is facilitated through meaningful interactions between locals and tourists who feel connected by co-learning practices. Duxbury and Bakas (2021) also suggest that as a result of their interaction, both visitors and locals are able to build their social capital. Previous definitions of creative tourism have emphasised the educational and skills development dimension (Richards & Raymond, 2000; UNESCO, 2006) or the exploration and expression of one's creative potential (Smith, 2016). However, literature on transformational tourism increasingly refers to deeper, more eudaimonic and spiritual dimensions which have the potential to change lives (Knobloch, Robertson, & Aitken, 2017; Matteucci, 2013; Reisinger, 2013; Sheldon, 2020). Enhancing one's creative skills and potential arguably forms part of meaningful and authentic life theories which encourage self-development and transformation (e.g. Seligman, 2002). Many retreat centres offer creative activities alongside more mindful and spiritual practices (Kelly & Smith, 2017).

Thirdly, Duxbury and Richards (2019) remark that in the last decade, young people's interest in developing their creative potential has kept on increasing, from 18% in 2012 to about 30% in 2017 (WYSE Travel Confederation, 2018). Since young people today will make up most of tomorrow's travellers, like Duxbury and Richards, we anticipate that the demand for creative tourism experiences is likely to grow in the future.

1.1 Contextualising the Demand for Creative Tourism Experiences

Creative tourism experiences do not take place in a vacuum. However, the social and physical contexts within which creative experiences are performed have remained largely underexplored. Examples might include slow cities in Italy, remote retreat destinations or even UNESCO creative cities. Throughout this book, we will seek to shed some light on the contextual forces that shape the creative tourist experience and on what it means and feels like to be a creative tourist within our modern world. The need to escape to slower, restorative, natural environments tends to encourage creative tourism, which also enables tourists to re-gain connection with themselves and their hidden or potential creativity. The modern world in which we live is marked by busy life-styles, fast transactions, great flows of people and things and boosted consumerism. These manifestations of the modern world have been linked to globalisation processes. Globalisation is a diffuse concept that is characterised by the removal of trade barriers (Stiglitz, 2002) and the fast movements of people, goods and capital, which are facilitated by technologies and have resulted in the emergence of a single world market dominated by multinational corporations. This fast-moving global market is driven by the economy, which shapes all spheres of human activities (Held, 1995), including tourism.

As the world becomes increasingly globalised, myriad cultural forms have become accessible to millions of tourists worldwide. Additionally, with the rise of mobility and easier access to information technologies, a multitude of previously silent voices are now being heard, new cultural expressions have emerged and old manifestations have been reshaped or simply revived. Not only do tourists travel to consume cultural resources, but also those resources themselves are becoming increasingly mobile, such as art exhibitions or music festivals. This has important implications for 'authenticity' of culture and context. De-contextualised (e.g. diasporic) or hybridised cultures may afford new opportunities. Along with the growing interest in culture, the resources associated with cultural tourism have expanded from the largely fixed, tangible heritage of the past towards the mobile, intangible products of contemporary culture (Richards, 2018). Therefore, within many cities, one can find as much cultural diversion at home as by going on holiday. This is beneficial for residents who can enjoy a diversity of cultural experiences on their doorstep, especially in large cities, but is less appealing for tourists seeking a sense of place and local cultural experiences. As a result of globalisation, tourism destinations have undergone a process of homogenisation (Ritzer, 2004), which occurs through standardisation and the reproduction of successful cultural attractions (e.g. Christmas markets, festivals and branded museums).

As a component of globalisation, tourism has grown to become an important contributor to the emergence of a global society (Munar, 2007), in which 'tourists are consumers, not anthropologists' (McKercher, 1993, p. 7). This portrayal of tourists as global consumers, rather than anthropologists, reveals tourism activities to be frivolous and tourism resources to be increasingly commodified. Indeed, the commodification of local cultures has been linked to the mass popularity gained by many destinations. Richards (2018) notes that, ironically, tourists often destroy the cultures that they seek to experience through travel. While the democratisation of heritage consumption and travel has arguably contributed to the commodification of cultures, four decades of neoliberal policies and poor tourism planning have also certainly left their mark on this issue (Matteucci et al., 2022). The failures of market neoliberalism, according to Monbiot (2016), are attributed to weaker government interventions, marketisation and privatisation of public space and services, tax breaks for the very rich, looser regulations, delocalisation of wealth and power and excessive individualism. Beyond governance issues, the last two decades have witnessed a shift in tourists' consumption of culture. On the one hand, tourists are now looking for to experience authenticity in the contemporary way of life of the places they visit (Frisch, Sommer, Stoltenberg, & Stors, 2019; Richards, 2011). On the other hand, many tourists are also 'actively and knowingly seeking the inauthentic as the basis of their experience' (Ravenscroft & Matteucci, 2003, p. 2). Smith (2016) describes these individuals as 'new leisure tourists'. A further complication may be their inability to distinguish what is authentic in a dynamic, globalising and hybridising world.

While some commentators (e.g. Franklin, 2003; Stebbins, 2006) have questioned the distinction between the activities carried out at home and those performed in tourism contexts, many scholars still see tourism activities as extraordinary either in terms of an escape from everyday life (Dann, 1977; Graburn, 1983; Wearing & Wearing, 1996) or as an opportunity to enact new roles (MacCannell, 2013) and adopt new identities (Desforges, 2000). In the context of the *escape* narrative, in need of relaxation, thrill and entertainment, many Western tourists find in tourism a space where they can 'let off steam' or abandon the restraints of their everyday environments (Fennell, 2000). In other words, the pressures experienced in modern societies oftentimes compel individuals to seek out new cultures and environments, new sensations, freedom and excitement that the monotony of their workaday life does not provide. Some tourists may even 'bypass' culture altogether as witnessed in the overtourism phenomenon in cultural cities, which is often connected to the night-time economy or party tourism. Increasingly, however (especially in the aftermath of the COVID-19 pandemic) tourists also crave a natural slow, quiet landscape in which they can recuperate away from the busyness of modern cities. Yet, it would be naive to believe that only jaded tourists travel to places. In recent years, the demand for more engaging, creative and meaningful experiences has been gaining momentum.

This trend may be explained by at least three main factors. Firstly, creative tourists have been associated with the values of the gentrifying new middle class who is attracted to destinations that are culturally diverse, boast modern or avant-garde amenities and offer culturally enriching experiences (Gretzel & Jamal, 2009; Ley, 1994). Secondly, as mobility has become ubiquitous and new technologies have become widely accessible, a new 'Creative Class' has emerged (Florida, 2002). Members of the Creative Class, Florida argues, include musicians, artists, teachers and scientists, and entrepreneurs from the creative industries (e.g. advertising, architecture, design and publishing). The Creative Class is, according to Florida, highly mobile and seeks out experiences that are aesthetically pleasurable, playful, active, intense and meaningful. Gretzel and Jamal (2009) suggest that the Creative Class is instilled with post-materialistic values, which drive them to pursue 'creative exploration of people, places, activities and things' (p. 476). Those creatives are cosmopolitans in that they are 'modern-day *flaneurs* who are comfortable walking the capitals' boulevards and flying short- and long haul-flights' (Skinner, 2007, p. 496). Like the descriptions of the Creative Class, cosmopolitans, according to Hannerz (1992), are skilled entrepreneurs and artisans with cultural know-how and 'a willingness to engage with the Other' (p. 252). Thirdly, the trend for creative tourism experiences is also explained by a rejection of mass tourism where experiences tend to be overly passive, superficial, standardised and commodified. Instead, tourists are increasingly concerned with creating their own experiences driven by 'learning by doing' and 'living like a local' (Richards, 2018). Richards (2021a) analyses the various 'turns' that have influenced cultural tourism from using culture as an economic and symbolic force to its performative and creative role. He argues that creative tourism could even be defined as a reaction to unengaging cultural tourism experiences in the context of globalisation, standardisation and serial reproduction. The performative and creative turn in cultural tourism connects to embodied and collaborative experiences, including rituals (Russo & Richards, 2016).

Our review of literature in creative tourism studies reveals that most discourses on creativity seem to uncritically present it as a valuable asset for residents and tourists alike. However, some disruptive voices, such as Korstanje et al. (2016), argue that creativity is another marketing trick deployed by capitalistic enterprises to lure alienated Western tourists into new forms of consumption, hence 'to boost marginal profits at lower costs' (p. 44). Exploring the hidden agendas of the tourism and cultural industries goes beyond the scope of this book; nevertheless, attending to issues of power relations and ethnocentrism behind the promise of creativity deserves scrutiny. In short, while the emphasis on creativity is on the rise in many spheres of social life, it remains unclear as to what creativity actually means?

1.2 Creativity

A cornerstone of creative tourism is creativity. Creativity is a fuzzy and contested concept. While creativity is something that many of us are looking for or experiencing in our daily life, it also sometimes means that some people have great ideas, which may result in the development of novel and useful products. In fact, creativity pervades all spheres of our everyday life from school assignments that require some creativity to compelling books that we read, fascinating films that we watch, and a wide range of innovative products and technologies that we enjoy using. However, most of the time, creativity may be experienced in more subtle and quiet ways. In his review of the work on creativity around the world, Sternberg (2006) shows that creativity is a multifaceted concept that is understood in variegated ways across cultures. For instance, in Scandinavian countries, creativity is construed as an attitude towards life and a way to cope with challenging situations. In the Chinese culture, creativity is associated with giftedness whereas in many Western countries, it is tied to sense of humour and aesthetic taste. Furthermore, Sternberg notes that, in French-speaking countries, creativity has been linked to imagination, while German speakers approach creativity as a solution to a problem. By way of further illustration, in African countries, creativity has been associated with adaptive social behaviour while in Turkey creativity is thought to stem from fantasy. This diversity of interpretations has led to many different approaches to studying creativity.

Scholars who have studied creativity agree on some general characteristics such as to make a creative contribution, the development of new knowledge and skills is necessary (Sternberg, 2006). In addition, creativity is commonly seen as a desirable quality, perhaps because creative individuals tend to enjoy above-average IQs (Baer & Kaufman, 2006) or because creativity has been associated with emotional well-being and self-actualisation (Simonton, 2000). The extensive work of Simonton (1988, 2000) on creativity indicates that creativity can be developed over the life-course and that some particular social environments and circumstances are fertile ground for its development. Since creativity can be developed – at least to some extent – researchers have been interested in understanding the factors that may stimulate its emergence. Among the many factors, which influence creativity, Sternberg includes personality traits, motivation, the social environment, relaxation, imagination, specific knowledge, expertise, cognitive styles and personal interest. With respect to personality, Baer and Kaufman (2006) report that a number of traits have been linked to creativity such as independence of judgement, self-confidence, attraction to complexity, aesthetic orientation, tolerance for ambiguity, openness to experience, risk taking and self-efficacy.

The literature on creativity underscores the complex set of factors that contribute to enhance someone's creative potential. Amongst others, Csikszentmihalyi (2014) has highlighted the need to pay attention to the intricate ways in which individuals interact within various contexts and society. To account for the emergence of creativity, Csikszentmihalyi suggests a system model, which consists of three main elements. The first of these three elements is the *domain* within which one operates. Each domain includes a set of conventions and procedures for action. The domain of art, for example, is made up of a plethora of artistic styles and movements, which can be considered sub-domains. The *field* is the second element, which includes 'all the individuals who act as gatekeepers to the domain' (p. 229). These gatekeepers are the experts who collectively decide what idea or product is worth adding to the domain. In the domain of art, Csikszentmihalyi notes, the field encompasses art critics, art historians, art collectors and artists themselves, among others. The third element is the *individual*. In the system model, Csikszentmihalyi argues that 'creativity occurs when a person makes a change in the information contained in a domain, a change that will be selected by the field for inclusion in the domain' (p. 229). The system model indicates that even though personality traits may promote creativity in one individual, it is only by attending to the other two elements that one may fathom the emergence of creativity. In this respect, Simonton (2006) remarks that although creativity clearly stems from social interactions, the social context within which creativity takes place has received little attention. Although psychologists are increasingly aware of the importance of social interactions in fostering creativity, they have tended to focus on the cognitive processes that lead to creative thought, thus neglecting the role of the body in creativity. Given the emphasis on *doing* in creative tourism, it would seem natural to attend to embodied ways of experiencing creativity. In fact, Creely, Henriksen, and Henderson (2020) remark that *embodied creativity* is a valuable concept for researching creativity in such fields as the performing arts and music where the sensuous body is fully engaged in the material world. The dynamic, embodied, relational character of creativity is encapsulated in Glăveanu's (2013) description of creativity as being 'concerned with the *action* of an *actor* or group of *actors*, in its constant interaction with multiple *audiences* and the *affordances* of the material world, leading to the generation of new and useful *artefacts*' (p. 76). By artefacts, Glăveanu means any visible expression in the form of objects, actions and performances; all of which are endowed with cultural meanings. For instance, in a dance improvisation workshop, Lucznik, May, and Redding (2021) have explored the influence of the socio-cultural environment on the development of movement creativity. These authors report that dancers were best able to unleash their creative potential in an environment promoting trust, in which they felt safe and accepted.

Joy Paul Guilford (1897–1987), an American psychologist, who has pioneered creativity research, asserts that everyone can show remarkable signs of creativity (and intelligence) in various contexts. Because a creative act is considered an instance of learning (Guilford, 1950) and because one can learn in multiple ways and contexts, creativity takes different shapes and forms such as everyday creativity, artistic creativity and intellectual creativity (Ivcevic & Mayer, 2009). Likewise, creativity manifests itself in a wide range of situations, from daily problem-solving at work and leisure to creative breakthroughs that may change the course of a particular domain. While creativity, mostly expressed in the form of learning and the acquisition of skills, is often developed during formal education, it can also be promoted informally during activities performed during leisure time (e.g. through craft-making).

Outside our everyday environment, tourism has become a vibrant venue for the stimulation of creativity through the development of skills, insights and performances (Richards, 2011). Richards and Wilson (2006) have reflected on the trends in the field of consumption in order to explain the growing demand for creativity in tourism. These commentators remark that individuals are not only increasingly dissatisfied with superficial modes of consumption, but creativity has also become attractive as a form of expression and for the construction of identities. The tourists' need for some creativity during a holiday may also be partly explained by the fact that people feel the intrinsic need to adjust to their ever-changing environment (Misra et al., 2006). The rigidity of routines and systems to which people feel obliged to conform stifle their daily creativity allowing few outlets for individual expression. Compounding this are political regimes that increasingly focus on compliance and surveillance, which further restrict peoples' freedom and silence their voices. Technology may also play a role in simultaneously enhancing and suppressing creativity. On the one hand, it enables interactivity and co-creation, on the other hand, it erodes precious time spent on passive pursuits that may be otherwise used for stimulating creativity. In addition, the rising interest in creative experience may be explained by the fact that creative and artistic activities are a conduit through which humans can thrive (Wright & Pascoe, 2015), understand themselves better (Berman, 1998) and improve their health (Clift & Camic, 2016).

Our cursory review of the literature on creativity has been largely influenced by studies within the field of psychology. Although psychology is primarily concerned with mental states and processes, the seminal and influential work of psychologists such as Guilford, Csikszentmihalyi, Sternberg and Simonton unambiguously points to the essential role of the social environment in fostering creativity in individuals. This observation calls for research practices that challenge the disciplinary silos and research traditions prevalent in tourist studies. We now turn to our philosophical position as researchers interested in understanding creative tourist experiences.

1.3 Our Philosophical Approach

Scholars writing about tourism draw inspiration from other scholars coming from a wide range of disciplines such as anthropology, sociology, psychology, history, cultural studies, management and marketing. This variety demonstrates the many facets of tourism scholarship and the many perspectives from which one can examine tourism phenomena. When tourism researchers draw from scholarly disciplines, they rely on conventions that are deeply rooted within these disciplines (Tribe, 2006). Conventions are value-laden and this implies that tourism scholars adhere to different ideas about the nature of reality (ontology), the nature of knowledge (epistemology), the role of ethics (axiology) and the ways knowledge can or should be produced; as a result, they follow multiple paths for producing this knowledge. Because tourism scholarship has been largely dominated by the cultures of management-oriented tourism schools (Hollinshead, 2004), knowledge produced by tourism researchers has often sought to meet the utilitarian goals of the tourism industry (Pearce, 2005). While seeking to solve the business problems of the tourism industry is laudable, we contend that tourism is more than just a mere industry. It seems that many advocates of the tourism industry often forget that the destinations they promote are places where people live. Because tourism is a complex socio-cultural phenomenon, the study of tourism, as Hannam and Knox (2010) remark, is 'always difficult and contested' (p. 3). We agree with the view that tourism is a multifaceted and complex phenomenon, and because the world is constantly changing, we see the need to embrace multiple and new ways of thinking about tourism. In our exploration of the creative tourist, we therefore draw inspiration from various disciplines as diverse as sociology, psychology, marketing and philosophy. Sociology is particularly useful because tourist experiences are always embedded within social contexts, hence we cannot ignore the power of social relations in shaping creative tourist experiences. We also draw on theories from psychology because an account of the creative tourist that did not attend to mental states, emotions and behaviours would not be satisfactory. In addition, even though social science research has largely been infused by the seminal work of ancient and modern thinkers, philosophy has been surprisingly scarce in tourism scholarship. We attempt to bridge this gap by incorporating concepts and ideas from thinkers who are closely or loosely associated with (new) materialist scholarship. New materialism scholarship encompasses a range of perspectives that underscore the relational, complex and pluralistic nature of the social world. New materialist scholars do not discard the human subject from their analysis; yet they recognise that human experience is always embodied and entangled with non-human materialities. In new materialist inquiry, non-human subjects (other species, objects and other materialities) are treated as equally agentic and important as the human subject. The wider political, economic and environmental context is, therefore, also taken into consideration because of the growth of neoliberal agendas that have impacted significantly on both destinations and their communities. Our work is placed in the context of the growing literature on transformative and regenerative tourism, which recognises the power of the individual tourist to take responsibility and to engage in creating a better world.

We adhere to the notion that creative tourism experiences – and any other form of knowledge – are constructed through social interaction. While we accept that there are some objective facts about the world, we believe that the way we experience the world is always subjective. In fact, we cannot experience the world beyond ourselves. Our philosophical position, therefore, is underpinned by constructivist epistemology. However, tourism experiences are also shaped through fluid human interactions in and with the physical world. This observation calls for acknowledging the complexity of human experience and the transversal forces that affect us in a variety of ways. In our effort to understand the creative tourist experience, we will draw from Gilles Deleuze's relational philosophy. Gilles Deleuze (1925–1995) is a French philosopher associated with post-structuralism and the materialist tradition. In Deleuzian thought, human beings and matter are entangled and both are ascribed agency in a non-hierarchical level of existence. In other words, the material world and the social world are viewed as intertwined and equally agentic, which intimates a more ethical vision of the world. In this vision of the world, humans are not superior to non-humans and all forms of life are intricately connected and interdependent. Deleuze's theorising resonates with the positions of materialist and new materialist thinkers such as Michel Onfray (1991, 2015) and Rosi Braidotti (2019). Materialism is a philosophical system that holds not only that everything is composed of matter – atoms – but that, fundamentally, all phenomena result from material interactions. French philosopher, Michel Onfray (2015) illustrates the materialist ontology as follows:

> The world, nature, birds, rivers, flowers, the moon and the sun, fish, plants, forests, plains, dogs, lights, colours, seasons, frogs, children, mice, dragonflies are all variations on the same theme: The cosmos. People are not separated from it, but in it. (pp. 429–430)

This connects closely to new theories of regenerative tourism, which are critical of the Anthropocene era and embrace a 'living systems' approach. Proponents advocate a more respectful and caring relationship between humans and nature (Dregde, 2022). The materialist ontology confers equal status and intrinsic value to both humans and non-human forms of life; it points to their fundamental interconnection and interdependency.

What are the key ideas that we find inspiring from Deleuze and the materialist tradition? Firstly, researchers should embrace the complexity of human experience in diverse social and natural contexts and they need to engage in dialogic exchange with their research participants and the social and physical world around them. By recognising the intersubjective nature of knowledge creation, we are cognizant that all actors, including the material world, are affecting and being affected by each other throughout the research process. For example, creative tourists engaged in cooking classes are impacted by other creative tourists, by local practitioners, by the physical environment as well as by a vast range of objects such as food stuff, but also smells and textures. Secondly, by giving the body an elevated status, any knowledge about creative experiences is co-constructed through discursive and embodied practices. This observation calls for sensual explorations of data through the research actors' bodies, which discern phenomena through the senses of smell, touch, sound and movement among other modalities (Matteucci & Gnoth, 2017). Thirdly, putting human and non-human actors on a same level of existence offers ways to think creatively beyond the lens of liberal humanism, whereby a host of inequalities, hierarchies and injustices may be revealed (Sterling, 2020).

To conclude, because we borrow ideas from various philosophical traditions (primarily social constructivism and materialism) and we embrace a multiplicity of theoretical and political dimensions, we see our scholarly work as *bricolage*. In French language, bricolage refers to the making of handiwork with whatever materials and tools are available. In social science research, proponents of bricolage (e.g. Berry, 2004; Denzin & Lincoln, 1999) see it as 'a critical, multi-perspectival, multi-theoretical and multi-methodological approach to inquiry' (Rogers, 2012, p. 1). In other words, bricolage entails the collapse of the boundaries between different disciplinary literatures, research methodologies and paradigms. In line with a bricolage mode of inquiry, we wrote this book by entering into a dialogue with creative tourists, with our own personal experiences of creative tourism activities, with an eclectic set of available information around tourism experiences including freshly collected data from the Vacation With An Artist internet platform (https://vawaa.com) and with the multidisciplinary literatures available to us. This book is not prescriptive; instead, we are aware that other paths may be followed in order to think and write about the creative tourist. While our endeavour presented here is certainly not flawless, we hope that our account of the creative tourist will resonate with a vast range of readers.

1.4 Book Outline

We see the creative tourist experience as a joyful journey full of sensual encounters and discoveries. Accordingly, we present an account of the creative tourist experience that connects multiple events, people and places. While the main protagonist who we are concerned with here is the creative tourist, there would be no creative tourism if there were no local residents, foreign cultures and exotic places. Throughout the chapters of this book, we seek to capture the multiplicity of factors, forces or intensities that shape the creative tourist experience. Because not all creative tourists share similar motives to travel and have similar immersive experiences, our account, therefore, is based on personal but also shared and available narratives that we believe are inspirational and deserve to be told. As a point of departure, Chapter 1 has outlined the rationale for the book and introduced globalisation and modernity as the broad contexts within which creative tourist experiences take place. Here, we have articulated our understanding of what creative tourism is and suggested that this participatory form of cultural tourism represents a regenerative alternative to mass cultural tourism. The complex and fluid concept of creativity is then discussed showing the multiple meanings and understandings of creativity across regions and academic disciplines. Because '[é]crire, c'est déjà choisir' [to write is to choose], as Camus (1951, p. 337) affirmed, we conclude this chapter by acknowledging the disciplinary knowledge and the philosophical movements that have inspired our scholarly endeavour.

Chapter 2 articulates the multiple dimensions of the tourist experience. It then situates the creative tourist within various tourist typologies and modes of experience, which are linked to the various motives that underlie tourists' participation in creative culture-based activities. In light of the performative turn in the social sciences, Chapter 3 discusses the important role of the body and senses in the creative tourist experience. Here, we suggest that attending to embodied practices sheds some light on the ways creative tourists negotiate their identities whereby differentiating themselves through the production or reproduction of cultural and/or economic capital.

Chapter 4 addresses the significant role of heterogeneous, creative tourism spaces in shaping tourist imaginaries, practices and experiences. While creative tourist spaces can be more or less contrived and regulated, we demonstrate that heterogeneous creative tourism environments are prone to stimulate strong emotions and offer imaginative and enacted alternatives to normative everyday spaces. We emphasise creative tourist spaces as liminoid for their transitional nature, and heterotopic for their disruptive capacity to affect those who dwell in them. Here, we explore the entanglement of moving bodies with the material and social worlds and argue that a sense of authenticity and intimacy are inherent qualities of creative tourist spaces. This chapter contributes to our understanding of the creative tourist space as a powerful epistemological concept that can inform us about processes of change, which are then brought to the fore in Chapter 5. It is here where we highlight that creative tourist spaces are conducive to enhanced well-being through empowerment, bonding, inspiration and self-transformation. We illustrate how the intimate socialities of some creative tourist spaces provide individuals with opportunities to explore their embodied identities as liberated tourists. Towards the end of Chapter 5, the creative tourist experience is presented as eudaimonic in character.

Our journey comes to an end in Chapter 6, which summarises the central themes and lessons drawn from this book. It is suggested that considering the creative tourist experience through a new materialist lens offers fresh perspectives on positive modes of becoming in the world. By adhering to an affirmative philosophy, which entails collaborative, embodied practices and rejects inertia, we propose to understand the creative tourist experience as a powerful source of inspiration in life, as a site of resistance, as a way to reclaim control over our lives, hence as an expansion of life capacities.

References

Argod, P. (2014). Art visuel et médiation d'un tourisme créatif: de l'Expérience du voyage, de la pratique artistique et des "créatifs culturels". *Mondes du Tourisme, 10*, 47–61. https://doi.org/10.4000/tourisme.378

Baer, J., & Kaufman, J. C. (2006). Creativity research in English-speaking countries. In J. Kaufman & R. J. Sternberg (Eds.), *The international handbook of creativity* (pp. 10–37). New York, NY: Cambridge University Press.

Bakas, F. E., Duxbury, N., & de Castro, T. V. (2018). Creative tourism: Catalysing artisan entrepreneur networks in rural Portugal. *International Journal of Entrepreneurial Behavior & Research, 25*(4), 731–752.

Berman, H. J. (1998). Creativity and aging: Personal journals and the creation of self. *Journal of Aging and Identity, 3*, 3–9. https://doi.org/10.1023/A:1022836604835

Berry, K. S. (2004). Structures of bricolage and complexity. In J. L. Kincheloe & K. S. Berry (Eds.), *Rigour and complexity in educational research: Conceptualizing the bricolage* (pp. 103–127). Ipswich, MA: Open University Press.

Braidotti, R. (2019). A theoretical framework for the critical posthumanities. *Theory, Culture & Society, 36*(6), 31–61. doi:10.1177/0263276418771486

Bryden, J., & Gezelius, S. J. (2017). Innovation as if people mattered: The ethics of innovation for sustainable development. *Innovation and Development, 7*(1), 101–118. doi:10.1080/2157930X.2017.1281208

Camus, A. (1951). *L'homme révolté*. Paris: Éditions Gallimard.

Clift, S., & Camic, P. (2016). *Oxford textbook of creative arts, health, and wellbeing: International perspectives on practice, policy and research*. Oxford: Oxford University Press.

Creely, E., Henriksen, D., & Henderson, M. (2020). Three modes of creativity. *The Journal of Creative Behavior, 55*, 306–318. doi:10.1002/jocb.452

Csikszentmihalyi, M. (2014). *The systems model of creativity: The collected works of Mihaly Csikszentmihalyi*. Dordrecht: Springer.

Dann, G. M. S. (1977). Anomie, ego-enhancement and tourism. *Annals of Tourism Research, 4*, 184–194. doi10.1016/0160-7383(77)90037-8

de Bruin, A., & Jelinčić, A. (2016). Toward extending creative tourism: Participatory experience tourism. *Tourism Review, 71*(1), 57–66. doi: 10.1108/TR-05-2015-0018

Denzin, N. K., & Lincoln, Y. S. (Eds.). (1999). *The SAGE handbook of qualitative research* (3rd ed.). London: Sage Publications.

Desforges, L. (2000). Traveling the world: Identity and travel biography. *Annals of Tourism Research, 27*(4), 926–945. https://doi.org/10.1016/S0160-7383(99)00125-5

Dredge, D. (2022). Regenerative tourism: Transforming mindsets, systems and practices. *Journal of Tourism Futures, 8*(3), 269–281. https://doi.org/10.1108/JTF-01-2022-0015

Duxbury, N., & Bakas, F. E. (2021). Creative tourism: A humanistic paradigm in practice. In M. Della Lucia & E. Giudici (Eds.), *Humanistic management and sustainable tourism: Human, social and environmental challenges* (pp. 111–131). London: Routledge.

Duxbury, N., & Richards, G. (2019). Towards a research agenda for creative tourism: Developments, diversity, and dynamics. In N. Duxbury & G. Richards (Eds.), *A research agenda for creative tourism* (pp. 1–14). Cheltenham: Edward Elgar Publishing.

Fennell, D. (2000). Tourism and applied ethics. *Tourism Recreation Research, 25*(1), 59–69. doi: 10.1080/02508281.2000.11014900

Florida, R. (2002). *The rise of the creative class and how it's transforming work, leisure, community and everyday life*. New York, NY: Basic Books.

Franklin, A. (2003). *Tourism: An introduction*. London: Sage.

Frisch, T., Sommer, C., Stoltenberg, L., & Stors, N. (2019). *Tourism and everyday life in the contemporary city*. London: Routledge.

Glăveanu, V. P. (2013). Rewriting the language of creativity: The five A's framework. *Review of General Psychology, 17*, 69–81. doi:10.1037/a0029528

Graburn, N. H. H. (1983). The anthropology of tourism. *Annals of Tourism Research, 10*(1), 9–33. doi:10.1016/0160-7383(83)90113-5

Gretzel, U., & Jamal, T. (2009). Conceptualizing the creative tourist class: Technology, mobility, and tourism experiences. *Tourism Analysis, 14*(4), 471–481. doi:10.3727/108354209X12596287114219

Guilford, J. P. (1950). Creativity. *American Psychologist, 5*, 444–454.

Hannam, K., & Knox, D. (2010). *Understanding tourism: A critical introduction*. London: Sage.

Hannerz, U. (1992). *Cultural complexity: Studies in the social organization of meaning*. Chichester: Columbia University Press.

Held, D. (1995). *Democracy and the global order: From the modern state to cosmopolitan governance*. Stanford, CA: Stanford University Press.

Hollinshead, K. (2004). A primer in ontological craft: The creative capture of people and place through qualitative research. In J. Phillimore & L. Goodson (Eds.), *Qualitative research in tourism: Ontologies, epistemologies and methodologies* (pp. 63–82). London: Routledge.

Ivcevic, Z., & Mayer, J. D. (2009). Mapping dimensions of creativity in the life-space. *Creativity Research Journal, 21*(1–2), 152–165. doi:10.1080/10400410902855259

Kelly, C., & Smith, M. K. (2017). Journeys of the self: The need to retreat. In M. K. Smith & L. Puczkó (Eds.), *The Routledge handbook of health tourism* (pp. 138–151). London: Routledge.

Knobloch, U., Robertson, K., & Aitken, R. (2017). Experience, emotion, and eudaimonia: A consideration of tourist experiences and well-being. *Journal of Travel Research, 56*(5), 651–662. doi:10.1177/0047287516650937

Korstanje, M., Echarri-Chavez, M., Cisneros Mustelier, L., & George, B. P. (2016). Creative tourism: Paradoxes and promises in the struggles to find creativity in tourism. *Journal of Tourism, 17*(2), 41–52.

Ley, D. (1994). Gentrification and the politics of the new middle class. *Environment and Planning D: Society and Space, 12*(1), 53–74. doi:10.1068/d120053

Lucznik, K., May, J., & Redding, E. (2021). A qualitative investigation of flow experience in group creativity. *Research in Dance Education, 22*(2), 190–209. doi:10.1080/1464 7893.2020.1746259

MacCannell, D. (2013). *The tourist: A new theory of the leisure class.* Berkeley, CA: University of California Press.

Matteucci, X. (2013). Experiencing flamenco: An examination of a spiritual journey. In S. Filep & P. Pearce (Eds.), *Tourist experience and fulfilment: Insights from positive psychology* (pp. 110–126). London: Routledge.

Matteucci, X. (2018). Expériences touristiques, flamenco et hapax existentiel. *Leisure/Loisir, 42*(2), 185–204. doi:10.1080/14927713.2018.1449133

Matteucci, X., & Gnoth, J. (2017). Elaborating on grounded theory in tourism research. *Annals of Tourism Research, 65*, 49–59. doi:10.1016/j.annals.2017.05.003

Matteucci, X., Nawijn, J., & von Zumbusch, J. (2022). A new materialist governance paradigm for tourism destinations. *Journal of Sustainable Tourism, 30*(1), 169–184. doi:10.1080/09669582.2021.1924180

McKercher, B. (1993). Some fundamental truths about tourism: Understanding tourism's social and environmental impacts. *Journal of Sustainable Tourism, 1*(1), 6–16. doi:10.1080/09669589309450697

Misra, G., Srivastava, A. K., & Misra, I. (2006). Culture and facets of creativity: The Indian experience. In J. Kaufman & R. J. Sternberg (Eds.), *The international handbook of creativity* (pp. 421–455). New York, NY: Cambridge University Press.

Monbiot, G. (2016). Neoliberalism – The ideology at the root of all our problems. *The Guardian.* https://www.theguardian.com/books/2016/apr/15/neoliberalism-ideology-problem-george-monbiot

Munar, A. M. (2007). Rethinking globalization theory in tourism. *Tourism, Culture & Communication, 7*, 99–115. doi:10.3727/109830407780339044

Onfray, M. (1991). *L'Art de jouir. Pour un matérialisme hédoniste.* Paris: Grasset.

Onfray, M. (2015). *Cosmos: Une ontologie matérialiste.* Paris: Flammarion.

Pearce, P. L. (2005). Professing tourism: Tourism academics as educators, researchers and change leaders. *The Journal of Tourism Studies, 16*(2), 21–33.

Ravenscroft, N., & Matteucci, X. (2003). The festival as carnivalesque: Social governance and control at Pamplona's San Fermin fiestas. *Tourism Culture & Communication, 4*(1), 1–15. doi:10.3727/109830403108750777

Reisinger, Y. (Ed.). (2013). *Transformational tourism: Tourist perspectives.* London: CABI.

Richards, G. (2011). Creativity and tourism: The state of the art. *Annals of Tourism Research, 38*(4), 1225–1253. doi:10.1016/j.annals.2011.07.008

Richards, G. (2018). Cultural tourism: A review of recent research and trends. *Journal of Hospitality and Tourism Management, 36*, 12–21. doi:10.1016/j.jhtm.2018.03.005

Richards, G. (2021a). *Re-thinking cultural tourism.* Cheltenham: Edward Elgar Publishing.

Richards, G. (2021b). Making places through creative tourism. In N. Duxbury (Ed.), *Cultural sustainability, tourism and development: (Re)articulations in tourism contexts* (pp. 36–48). London: Routledge.

Richards, G., & Raymond, C. (2000). Creative tourism. *ATLAS News, 23*, 16–20.

Richards, G., & Wilson, J. (2006). Developing creativity in tourist experiences: A solution to the serial reproduction of culture? *Tourism Management, 27*, 1209–1223. doi:10.1016/j.tourman.2005.06.002

Ritzer, G. (2004). *The globalization of nothing*. London: Sage.

Rogers, M. (2012). Contextualizing theories and practices of bricolage research. *The Qualitative Report, 17*(7), 1–17.

Russo, A. P., & Richards, G. (Eds.). (2016). *Reinventing the local in tourism*. Bristol: Channel View.

Scherf, K. (2021). Creative tourism in smaller communities: Collaboration and cultural representation. In K. Scherf (Ed.), *Creative tourism in smaller communities: Place, culture and local representation* (pp. 1–26). Calgary: University of Calgary Press.

Seligman, M. E. P. (2002). *Authentic happiness*. New York, NY: Free Press.

Sheldon, P. (2020). Designing tourism experiences for inner transformation. *Annals of Tourism Research, 83*, 102935. doi:10.1016/j.annals.2020.102935

Simonton, D. K. (1988). *Scientific genius: A psychology of science*. New York, NY: Cambridge University Press.

Simonton, D. K. (2000). Creativity: Cognitive, personal, development, and social aspects. *American Psychologist, 55*, 151–158. https://doi.org/10.1037/0003-066X.55.1.151

Simonton, D. K. (2006). Creativity around the world in 80 ways … but with one destination. In J. Kaufman & R. J. Sternberg (Eds.), *The international handbook of creativity* (pp. 490–496). New York, NY: Cambridge University Press.

Skinner, J. (2007). The salsa class: A complexity of globalization, cosmopolitans and emotions. *Identities: Global Studies in Culture and Power, 14*, 485–506. doi:10.1080/10702890701578480

Smith, M. K. (2016). *Issues in cultural tourism studies* (3rd ed.). London: Routledge.

Stebbins, R. A. (2006). *Serious leisure: A perspective for our time*. Somerset, NJ: Aldine Transaction Publications.

Sterling, C. (2020). Critical heritage and the posthumanities: Problems and prospects. *International Journal of Heritage Studies, 26*(11), 1029–1046. doi:10.1080/1352725 8.2020.1715464

Sternberg, R. J. (2006). Introduction. In J. Kaufman & R. J. Sternberg (Eds.), *The international handbook of creativity* (pp. 1–9). New York, NY: Cambridge University Press.

Stiglitz, J. (2002). *Globalization and its discontents*. New York, NY: W. W. Norton & Company.

Tribe, J. (2006). The truth about tourism. *Annals of Tourism Research, 33*(2), 360–381. doi:10.1016/j.annals.2005.11.001

UNESCO. (2006). Discussion report of the planning meeting for 2008. In *International conference on creative tourism*, October 25–27, Sante Fe, New Mexico.

Wearing, B., & Wearing, S. (1996). Refocussing the tourist experience: The flâneur and the choraster. *Leisure Studies, 15*, 229–243. doi:10.1080/026143696375530

Wright, P. R., & Pascoe, R. (2015). Eudaimonia and creativity: The art of human flourishing. *Cambridge Journal of Education, 45*(3), 295–306. doi:10.1080/0305764X. 2013.855172

WYSE Travel Confederation. (2018). *New horizons IV*. Paris: UNWTO and UNESCO.

Chapter 2

Dimensions of the Creative Tourist Experience

The focus of this chapter is on the multiple dimensions of the creative tourist experience. An exploration of the creative tourist experience first requires a brief discussion of various perspectives on the more general tourist experience, different types of tourists and the variegated modes of experience relevant to tourism activities. This chapter, therefore, commences with a discussion of the concepts of *experience* and of *the tourist experience*, then proceeds to examine categorisations of tourism experiences. Following this introduction, we will focus on the creative tourist experience in terms of motivation and the tourists' perspectives on creativity.

The word experience is frequently used in everyday language to describe life events of all kinds. While the emphasis on experience in tourism advertisement is visible through the abundant use of experiential verbs such as discover, explore, feel or sense, the notion of experience has also become a key element in understanding the ethical issues and welfare issues related to tourism activities (Hall & Brown, 2006) and more generally in furthering human quality of life and well-being (Filep, Moyle, & Skavronskaya, 2022; Pearce, 2009; Pearce, Filep, & Ross, 2011). The everyday usage of the word experience covers two related meanings: first, experience is 'the process of observing or perceiving, sensing, encountering or undergoing some event'; and second, it is associated with learning and the practical knowledge gained from life encounters (Moscardo, 2009, p. 99). The former type of experience is often linked to the activities of travel, tourism and adventure and is generally referred to as a source of intense stimulation (Lash, 2006). The latter type more generally alludes to the empirical knowledge gained through living life, experiences that make one more mature, wiser and better informed. Both usages of the term experience are related in that they both entail that experience is something that is personal in nature and happens within the self. Therefore, an experience cannot be felt or reproduced in the same fashion outside the self (Bruner, 1986).

Unlike the English, French and Spanish languages among others, the German language enjoys two different expressions that convey the notion of experience.

The Creative Tourist: A Eudaimonic Perspective, 17–33
Copyright © 2024 by Xavier Matteucci and Melanie Kay Smith
Published under exclusive licence by Emerald Publishing Limited
doi:10.1108/978-1-83753-404-320241002

These are *Erfahrung* and *Erlebnis*. According to Lash (2006), Erfahrung is a cognitive experience, which relates to the idea of physical encounter. The action described in the verb erfahren corresponds to the accumulation of knowledge, or sense making. In contrast to Erfahrung, Erlebnis and its verbal form *erleben* are connected with the realm of feeling. By associating Erlebnis with an aesthetic and metaphysical experience, German poet and philosopher Friedrich Schiller (1759–1805) is said to have been the first to differentiate the two expressions (Lash, 2006). Both modalities of experience are interrelated and constituent of the self. Indeed, Larsen (2007) asserts that by engaging in various activities while on holiday (Erlebnis), tourists accumulate memories, and hence knowledge (Erfahrung). Beyond the subtleties of the Erfahrung and Erlebnis distinction, the human experience in its wholeness is, therefore, not fixed. Instead, 'it is a process in which there are a number of possibilities that arise within or through a particular situation' (Andrews, 2009, p. 9). The non-fixity of the tourist experience is also underscored by Kang and Gretzel (2012) who define it as 'a constant flow of thoughts and feelings during moments of consciousness, which occur through highly complex psychological, sociological and cognitive interaction processes' (p. 442). Beyond the definitions provided by social scientists, the personal character and the fluidity of experience have been highlighted by a number of philosophers such as Gilles Deleuze (2002) who conceives the embodied experience as a centre of intensities that are affected by the multiple and unpredictable forces of the world; a point that we will address in more detail in Chapter 3 of this book.

French sociologist Rachid Amirou (1995) distinguishes what he considers to be three major realms of the tourist's life world, namely: the relationship to self, to space and to others. These three realms, he claims, are shaped by the tourist's imagination, for instance, her/his real or fantasised ideas of the spaces visited, of the populations inhabiting these spaces and of their relationships to others in these spaces. Thus, worldviews, but also human experiences, are influenced by the tourist's imagination, which is shaped by the ideology and the myths of the society to which the tourist belongs. Ryan (2010) illustrates the complex and multifaceted nature of the tourist experience when he writes that

> [it] is shaped by many things, motive, past experience, knowledge of place, persons with whom that place is shared, patterns of change at the place, the images induced about place and activities, individual personalities – so it seems that to study the tourist experience is of necessity a study of individual stories that, as researchers, one records, assesses and passes on – not as definitive assessments of truth, but as sources that inform evaluations of others' experiences. (p. 44)

Some researchers have associated tourism with a kind of modern pilgrimage (Cohen, 1979; Graburn, 1989) where tourists seek the authentic in an exotic and foreign *Other* (MacCannell, 2013). This quest for the other sometimes denotes a spiritual approach as in the example of ashram stays, punctuated by the practice of yoga, meditation and the discovery of others as well as the sharing of experiences (Sharpley & Sundaram, 2005). Some spirituality can also be experienced during leisure activities such as walking (Maddrell, 2011; Saunders, Laing, & Weiler, 2013), reading, horseback riding, climbing and gardening (Schmidt & Little, 2007), performing batá drumming (Windress, 2016) and practicing flamenco dance and music (Matteucci, 2013). Willson, McIntosh and Zahra's (2013) study, for example, reports that in the context of a trip to Peru, spirituality manifests itself in transcendental experiences, a sense of connection to the world and the search for meaning. Beyond the common idea that leisure and, by extension, tourism, is fuelled by the need for relaxation, entertainment and personal development, travel seems to correspond more to a quest for meaning or the search for happiness. In this regard, Urbain (2007) views travel or any movement to other spaces as a transplantation, that is, an 'opportunity to become other or to become oneself' (p. 24). Before Urbain, Amirou (1995) noted that French philosopher Gaston Bachelard (1943) alluded to the symbolic death of the individual from the moment she/he goes on a journey. In other words, in leaving her/his place of residence, the traveller becomes another person. Michel de Montaigne is cited as saying that instead of being enclosed within ourselves, the world affords us a mirror in which to see ourselves and to know ourselves (Rigolot, 1992). It allows travellers to see the world differently as well as enhance sense of self (Santayana, 1964).

2.1 Tourist Typologies

Many tourism scholars (e.g. Cohen, 1974, 1979; Crompton, 1979; Dann, 1977; Pearce, 1982; Plog, 1987; Sharpley, 1994) have sought to categorise tourists based on their experiences and motives for travel. A widely cited tourist typology is the one from sociologist Erik Cohen (1979) who presents a spectrum of five modes of experience based on a quest for pleasure at one end and a search for meaning at the other. The nature of the quest, Cohen argues, depends on the tourists' degree of alienation from their everyday routine and their level of interest in the foreign *Other*. These five tourist types are defined as 'recreational', 'diversionary', 'experiential', 'experimental' and 'existential'. In the *recreational* mode of experience, tourists seek to experience pleasure through entertainment. In the *diversionary* mode, individuals need a break away from their workaday life and stress in order to maintain life-balance. The *experiential* mode of experience intimates that, because people are conscious of their state of alienation, they seek out more authentic experiences elsewhere. The *experimental* tourists are similarly alienated but go on a quest to discover who they really are in an exotic environment. Lastly, *existential* tourists are individuals who believe that they would live happier lives elsewhere. The existential tourists, therefore, wish to temporarily or permanently relocate to foreign places. Even more than the other modes of experience, the existential mode is replete with desires and fantasies, and with romantic and nostalgic associations of exotic cultures. While Cohen's typology may be useful in pointing to the diversity and plurality of tourist experiences, it fails to provide

a nuanced account of gender issues, cultural diversity (Uriely, 2005), power relations, conflicts of interest and inequalities (Wearing, Stevenson, & Young, 2010).
In addition, tourist typologies, such as Cohen's (1979), have been criticised for not
attending to the voices and perspectives of the tourist (Wearing & Wearing, 2001)
and for not considering that tourists may shift position along this continuum as
they progress through their trip (Steiner & Reisinger, 2006).

These ideas have been partly followed up by cultural and creative tourism
scholars who have developed segmentation models based on 'travel careers' or
'destination journeys' (Richards, 2021). These incorporate ideas of 'omnivorous-
ness' (Peterson, 1992) or the simultaneous consumption of different cultural
activities and experiences. The segmentation models combine age, life-stage,
gender and preferred experiences. For example, it was noted that Generation Y
women and men tend to prefer experiences to possessions, especially creative
experiences; older travellers gravitate more towards educational experiences
than younger generations who prefer entertaining experiences (Richards, 2021);
Generation Z, meanwhile, might be more likely to search for authentic 'back-of-
house' experiences (McKercher, 2020).

Recognising that tourist types of experiences are not mutually exclusive and
that tourists may switch from one mode to another during the same holiday, Gnoth
and Matteucci (2014) suggest a typology, referred to as the Tourism Experience
Model (TEM), which is based on the premise that experiences are a function
of consciousness and activity. These authors distinguish four modes of experiencing, namely: experience as 'pure pleasure', as 're-discovery', as 'existentially
authentic exploration', and as 'knowledge seeking'. Experience as *pure pleasure* is
when tourists engage in activities that are habitual and familiar and that are self-
directed. While the site or attraction they visit may be a point of interest, their
pursuit is hedonistic in that tourists are more concerned with the pleasure derived
from being there; however, this experience may be highly meaningful to them. The
re-discovery mode of experiencing entails that tourists purposively participate in
activities that necessitate some focus and effort (e.g. learning to play African percussion). In this mode, the tourist self is fulfilled beyond mere indulgence. In the
experiencing mode of *existentially authentic exploration*, the tourist's focus is not
self-directed as in the two previous modes, but other-directed. In the course of
their exploration of exotic environment, communities and cultures, tourists are
confronted with unusual and challenging situations that may lead them to negotiate their own identities. In this process, tourists may feel transformed which,
in turn, may give rise to new life trajectories. The fourth mode of experiencing – *knowledge seeking* – is also other-directed. It posits that, although they are
motivated to learn new things, tourists follow normative scripts and roles in order
to protect their ego. For example, in the case of a visit to a museum, tourists
would seek out new experiences, albeit from their own socio-culturally familiar
lenses. Gnoth and Matteucci (2014) argue that these four modes of experiencing
may be interwoven throughout the tourist journey, thus alternating participation
in activities that are either self-directed or other-directed.

While Cohen's (1979) typology simplistically identified the qualities attributed to various tourists (Wearing, Stevenson, & Young, 2010), the value of the

TEM is that it more adequately captures the characteristics of tourist practices and modes of experiencing. Furthermore, the four modes of experiencing that make up the TEM seem to accommodate well the fluid consumption practices that define the postmodern world, a world in which some tourists shift their consumption practices in an attempt to resist the pressure from capitalist commodification (Wearing et al., 2010). Finally, following Saraniemi and Kylänen's (2011) observation, it may be argued that the TEM reflects the behaviour of contemporary 'mobile tourists who want to experience diverse themes, and take various, or even contrasting, roles as consumers and producers and cannot therefore be reduced to generalised targets with predictable, permanent consumption preferences' (p. 140). While the TEM may help to better distinguish the processes of experiencing (Gnoth & Matteucci, 2014), it still fails to unearth important issues of gender, identity construction, power relations and social justice that impact the self. Given that a nuanced understanding of the creative tourist experience is our focal point, we believe it is essential to direct our attention on the qualities of the creative experience. By so doing, we will explore the motives that underlie tourists' practices, how tourists experience their activities and we will seek to understand the meaning people ascribe to what they do. These are the concerns of the subsequent chapters.

2.2 The Creative Tourist

In our earlier discussion of the context within which creative tourism takes place, we have alluded to the emergence of a new Creative Class (Florida, 2002), which comprises people who are curious about the world and who seek out aesthetic and life-transforming experiences (Gretzel & Jamal, 2009). Moreover, members of the Creative Class are said to be looking for places that are characterised by great cultural diversity, tolerance, talent and technology. Yet, the idea that creative tourists are members of the Creative Class, as conceptualised by Richard Florida, seems to be more taken for granted than substantiated, as there is no empirical evidence to date that can attest to this assumption. Indeed, the occupational profiles of the Creative Class has been subject to much debate across disciplines. Some authors (e.g. Krätke, 2010) have questioned the delimitations of the Creative Class in terms of the subgroups that make up this concept. Florida (2002) asserts that the Creative Class are people belonging to three different occupational groups, namely the 'highly creative', the 'bohemians' and the 'creative professionals'. The *highly creative* are described as those working in engineering, information sciences, economics and the social sciences, architecture, health sciences and other academic disciplines. The *bohemians* consist of individuals working in the cultural sector such as writers, visual and performing artists, musicians, designers and handicraft artisans. A much-contested category is the *creative professionals* that Florida presents as a heterogeneous group, which includes qualified technicians, consultants, brokers and those working in the fields of finance, real-estate, social and health services, as well as politics. Krätke (2010) and Jesus, Kamlot, and Dubeux (2020), among others, have questioned the professed mobilisation of creativity in the work of the so-called creative professionals. To illustrate this point of contention, Krätke (2010) argues that '[b]y using a rather nebulous idea of creativity, Florida presents a concept of social classes based on arbitrary assignments and supports a self-idealisation of the "leading" occupational groups of today's capitalism' (p. 836). Florida has not only failed to convince of the nature of creativity in the tasks performed by those labelled as creative professionals, but the association between the creative professionals, tolerance and sustainable economic development has not been ascertained (Krätke, 2010). In short, merely assimilating creative tourists to the Creative Class appears to be rather speculative, therefore, examining the links between creative tourists and the different subgroups of the Creative class in terms of their demographic and occupational profiles, deserves some further scrutiny.

While few empirical studies have specifically examined who the creative tourists are, the wide literature on creative tourism has presented some general defining characteristics of the creative tourist. Creative tourists have been described as individuals who are looking for authentic experiences, for self-development through active participation in cultural activities and for opportunities to develop their creative potential (Binkhorst, 2007; Remoaldo, Serra, Marujo, Alves, Gonçalves, Cabeça, & Duxbury, 2020; Richards, 2011; Richards & Wilson, 2006). Furthermore, Gretzel and Jamal (2009) have argued that creative tourists are 'empowered consumers' in search of aesthetic experiences 'through embodied, physical engagement with the environment and with technologies' (p. 477). A salient aspect of creative tourism is the high degree of agency that the tourist exerts in crafting her/his own experience (de Bruin & Jelinčić, 2016). Empowerment and agency are reflected in the term 'prosumer' (a fusion of the terms *producer* and *consumer* or *professional consumer*), which has been used to refer to the creative tourist (e.g. Richards & Wilson, 2006). In contrast to the more passive mode of consumption that characterises the modern consumers of the post-industrial era, prosumers are individuals who are actively producing the products and experiences they consume (Toffler, 1980). Arguably, technological advancements, such as the use of Web 2.0, have accelerated the development of prosumption, which some commentators have associated with new forms of free labour and exploitation (Jemielniak & Przegalinska, 2020). Because the term prosumption intimates a business philosophy that expects consumers to dedicate time and efforts in producing something without getting paid, prosumption does not really capture what creative tourism is about. Instead, given the importance of interpersonal encounters and the learning opportunities sought after through creative tourism, the term *co-creation* more adequately conveys the participative cultural experiences that are performed by creative tourists. Richards and Marques (2018) describe creative development as a system of co-creation, which requires the involvement and collaboration of all of those who visit, use and live in a place. Thus, in the process of creative place-making, tourists become 'essential actors in the co-creation of place, re-negotiating meanings of place that attract them' (Richards, 2020, p. 4).

What kinds of cultural activities are creative tourists pursuing? The cultural heritage resources that creative tourists travel to experience include, but are not limited to, theatre, literature, painting, sculpture, poetry, music, cinema, dance, architecture, storytelling, food, street art and folklore. Table 2.1 provides some examples

Table 2.1. Examples of Creative Tourism Activities.

Cultural Activities in CT	Context	Authors
Bone carving (jewellery making)	Maori tradition (New Zealand)	Raymond (2007)
Wooden furniture and pottery making	Taiwan	Tan, Kung, and Luh (2013)
Pottery, craft, art workshops	Taiwan	Chang, Backman, and Chih Huang (2014)
Poetry reading	Macau	Zhang and Xie (2019)
Thai cooking classes	Chiang Mai (Thailand)	Suntikul, Agyeiwaah, Huang, and Pratt (2020)
Thai cooking classes	Bangkok (Thailand)	Walter (2017)
Thai cooking classes	Thailand	Mills (2019)
Wood carving, dance and Gamelan practices, cooking classes, farming	Bali (Indonesia)	Blapp and Mitas (2018)
Home cooking classes	Bali (Indonesia)	Bell (2015)
Silk-weaving	Japan	Creighton (1995)
Cooking classes	Tatarstan (Russia)	Aksenova, Cai, and Gebbels (2022)
Re-enactments and artworks of archaeological heritage sites	Alentejo (Portugal)	Ross and Saxena (2019)
Harvesting and wine making	Barraida (Portugal)	Carvalho, Kastenholz, and Carneiro (2021)
Traveloging and travel book sketching	Multiples sites (e.g. Bretagne)	Argod (2014)
Cooking workshops	Barcelona (Catalunya)	Ilinčić (2014)
Flamenco dance and music classes	Seville, Andalusia (Spain)	Matteucci (2012, 2013, 2014, 2018a, 2018b) and Matteucci and Filep (2017)

(Continued)

Table 2.1.   (*Continued*)

Cultural Activities in CT	Context	Authors
Salsa dance classes	Cuba	Menet (2020)
Batá drumming	Cuba	Windress (2016)
Cooking classes and salsa dance classes	Colombia	Zuluaga and Guerra (2021)
Craft and chocolate making	Brazil and Peru	Dias, González-Rodriguez, and Patuleia (2021)
Music, dance and percussion workshops	Siby (Mali)	Marques (2012)
West African dance (Sabar) classes	Senegal	Aterianus-Owanga (2019) and Bizas (2014)
Sufi dance classes, calligraphy, cooking classes	Marrakech (Morocco)	Reda Khomsi and Safaa (2015)
Amulet making and clay pottery	Sante Fe, New Mexico (USA)	Wurzburger, Aageson, Pattakos and Pratt (2010)
Bread making, canvas mat making, etc.	Newfoundland (Canada)	Hull and Sassenberg (2012)

of creative tourism studies including the cultural activities and the context within which these activities take place. It should be noted, however, that even if the types of activities undertaken by tourists unambiguously fit the creative tourism concept, many authors do not necessarily refer to their work as creative tourism.

2.3 Motives for Participation in Creative Tourism

Some tourism researchers have attempted to define and categorise creative tourists. For example, the Creative Tourism Network includes artists such as those travelling to give a performance and to hold workshops, as well artists in residence (artists given space and resources to develop their artistic practices). Even more broadly, Raymond (2003) suggests that creative tourists can be anyone interested in learning something about the local culture while on holiday. These descriptions are rather broad and do not clearly inform about the types of experiences people undergo and the motives that underlie creative experiences. Three more thorough attempts at categorising creative tourists come from Tan et al. (2014), Remoaldo et al. (2020) and Zuluaga and Guerra (2021). Based on a Taiwanese sample, Tan et al. (2014) identified five different groups, namely 'novelty-seekers', 'knowledge and skills learners', those who are 'aware of travel partners' growth', those who are 'aware of green issues' and the 'relax and leisure type' (p. 257). The *novelty-seekers* are people attracted by new activities, and for these tourists, creativity is linked to novelty. As the terms indicate, the *knowledge and skills learners* consist of individuals who are primarily seeking to expand their knowledge and skills through challenging activities. The fact that a creative cultural activity requires some effort is valuable to them. *Aware of travel partners' growth* are those who select learning activities that will contribute to the personal development of their travel companions, such as children. For these creative tourists, Tan et al. (2014) argue that hygiene and a friendly and inspiring tutor are important factors. Those who belong to the *aware of green issues* category are people concerned with eco-friendly activities and activities that contribute to the preservation of the intangible cultural heritage of the destination. Lastly, the *relax and leisure type* of creative tourists include those who seek to escape their everyday routine, have fun and find some rest. Those tourists emphasise the importance of the physical and atmospheric qualities of the spaces within which creative activities are performed.

In the context of small and medium-sized cities and rural areas of Portugal, Remoaldo et al. (2020) identified three similar clusters of creative tourists, namely 'novelty-seekers', 'knowledge and skills learners' and 'leisure creative-seekers'. The *novelty-seekers* are described to be primarily looking for fun, new and creative activities. Accompanying someone or meeting new people as well as expanding their cultural knowledge are the core motives behind the *knowledge and skills-seekers*. The *leisure creative-seekers* emphasise the importance of social encounters and the co-creation of experiences. While these categories differentiate creative tourists based on one core motive, it should be noted that these categories are not fixed and they are not mutually exclusive. In other words, motivation is multilayered, whereby multiple motives may often underpin participation in creative tourism. Rich of their seven-year experience operating a creative tourism business in Bogota, Zuluaga and Guerra (2021) identify three main demographic groups of creative tourists, namely adults aged 30–45, adults aged 46–60 and families. A common denominator in these three groups is their desire to 'share intimately with a local host, a place that allows the traveller to feel as immersed as possible in the culture of their chosen destination' (p. 15).

The motivation-based typology of creative tourists devised by Tan et al. (2014) expands on these authors' previous endeavour to understand the essence of creativity that tourists seek in creative tourism. Firstly, as a point of departure, Tan et al. (2013) present the creative experience as a function of 'outer interactions' with the social and physical environments and 'inner reflections' about the tourists' intrinsic needs for creativity. This process of the creative experience resembles the TEM articulated by Gnoth and Matteucci (2014), who posit that the tourist experience is a function of consciousness (inner reflections) and activity (outer interactions). While the experiential modes of the TEM may relate to different types of tourism experiences in general, Tan et al. (2013) argue that tourists' consciousness/awareness (inner reflections) is a prerequisite for a tourism experience to be classified as creative. What is meant by consciousness/awareness is that tourists are not only reflective of their own personal needs (e.g. social encounters and interaction, cultural learning) but they are also more attuned to the social and natural contexts within which creative activities are embedded. Secondly, based on the tourists' inner reflections and interactions with the world, Tan et al. (2013) suggest that creativity manifests itself in various ways. Creativity, they argue, may correspond to a need for novelty, usefulness, challenge, pleasure and self-transformation.

While *novelty* is often seen as a basic ingredient of any experience away from one's usual environment, creativity as *usefulness* is a prevalent aspect of the creative tourist experience. For instance, tourists may be aspiring to gain some specific skills through creative tourism in order to perform some activities back home. This aspect of creativity is apparent in the tourist experience of flamenco dance and music, as reported in Matteucci's (2012) work with creative tourists in Seville. Many flamenco tourists had consciously and unambiguously articulated the need to gain some knowledge and improve their cultural and motor skills in order to use their newly acquired skills in their professional careers back home.

The following quote from Aaron, an American guitar player, reveals his eagerness to learn from Andalusian flamenco artists in order to improve his skills in guitar playing:

> I mean if this is what you want to do, it has to be the number one priority because if it's not – and that's fine, people don't have it as a number priority and they just enjoy going to classes and things. But you know, this is what I do when I'm back in the States. And what I want to do for a long time, and I want to teach, and try to make a living out of it. And so the only way that I can do that is to make it a number one priority. (p. 135)

The phrases 'a number one priority' and 'make a living out of it' point to Aaron's drive to acquire the skills that he will need in order to perform flamenco professionally in the United States. The type of skills that creative tourists like Aaron are looking for are specialist skills, that is, a set of high skills that are context-dependent, gained through practice and guided by local experts. The mastery of flamenco, whether in the form of dance or music skills, can be interpreted as a form of 'physical capital' – 'something that has an exchange value within a metaphorical economy' (Hannam & Knox, 2010, p. 59). The Vacation With An Artist internet platform also provides some examples of creativity as usefulness. For instance, in the context of a traditional weaving and dyeing course in Vietnam, Kim Marie describes her educational motive in the following terms:

> It is my hope that I can one day soon, I will be confident and enough to share the traditional skills of planting, growing and extracting indigo/dye with the students I teach here in Hanoi, in order to inspire them to become the ethical designers of tomorrow.

Creativity as *challenge* is another key aspect of the creative tourist experience. The tourists' willingness to be confronted with some form of challenge can be explained by the creative tourists' central concern with learning new skills. To reach the educational goals they have set for themselves, creative tourists sometimes venture into the unknown. For instance, in Matteucci's (2012) study, some creative tourists had quit their well-paid jobs to live their passion for flamenco and had exposed themselves to an uncertain future. The flamenco enthusiasts reported hard times, which they expressed with words and phrases such as *sacrifice, hard work, discipline, pressure, pain* and living on a *tight budget*. Below the words articulated by Maya exemplify the creative experience as challenge:

> It is daily hard work – work of many daily hours. Every day, that means, if it is every day, it means perseverance as time goes by. Physical perseverance and I mean also psychological; bearing down. (p. 233)

Another example of the type of challenges faced by some creative tourists is physical pain as illustrated below by Natalie:

> And I've been living in flip-flops for like two months and three weeks ago my feet weren't used to be enclosed. And we do a lot of those like technique classes. We do a lot of twisting and stuff, so it's like it feels that my feet are bruised because I've been working so much. The girl I am meeting later, Jessica, she already has a week of dancing and her feet are kind of sprained right now too. She's having a real hard time with it. (p. 191)

The acquisition of new skills and knowledge often requires some efforts and dedication, which at times can be demanding. While creative activities can be strenuous, these activities may also be perceived to be enjoyable. Creativity as *pleasure* is, therefore, another salient aspect of the creative tourist experience.

Table 2.2.   Motives Underlying Participation in Creative Tourism.

Motives	Authors
Novelty/surprise	Creighton (1995), Matteucci (2012), Remoaldo et al. (2020), Paschinger (2021), Tan et al. (2014) and Zuluaga and Guerra (2021)
Relaxation	Dean and Suhartanto (2019), Matteucci (2012) and Tan et al. (2014)
Self-development (learning)	Argod (2014), Bizas (2014), Carvalho et al. (2021), Ilinčić (2014), Matteucci (2012, 2018a), Matteucci and Filep (2017), Menet (2020), Reda Khomsi and Safaa (2015), Remoaldo et al. (2020), Richards and Wilson (2006), Skinner (2016), Smith (2016), Tan et al. (2014), Windress (2016), Zhang and Xie (2019) and Zuluaga and Guerra (2021)
Mastery (honing professional skills)	Matteucci (2012) and Menet (2020)
Preservation of intangible heritage	Reda Khomsi and Safaa (2015) and Tan et al. (2014)
Escape everyday routine	Creighton (1995), Dean and Suhartanto (2019), Matteucci (2012) and Zhang and Xie (2019)
Fun/enjoyment/play	Dean and Suhartanto (2019), Matteucci (2012) and Mills (2019)
Authentic experiences	Bizas (2014), Creighton (1995), Gombault (2014), Matteucci (2012, 2018b), Richards and Wilson (2006) and Zhang and Xie (2019)
Social encounters	Bizas (2014), Ilinčić (2014), Matteucci (2012), Menet (2020), Remoaldo et al. (2020), Paschinger (2021), Tan et al. (2014), Zhang and Xie (2019) and Zuluaga and Guerra (2021)
Dream realisation	Matteucci (2012)
Life-balance	Matteucci (2012)
Add cultural value to their travel experience	Mills (2019)
Remedy a lack of self-esteem	Matteucci (2014)
Self-expression and self-exploration	Argod (2014), Matteucci (2014), Skinner (2007) and Skinner (2016)
(Re)negotiation of cultural and self-identities	Argod (2014), Creighton (1995), Jelinčić and Senkić (2019), Matteucci (2014), Menet (2020), Mills (2019) and Skinner (2007)
Self-transformation	Matteucci (2012, 2018b, 2022) and Tan et al. (2014)

To illustrate the experience of pleasure, we draw from two quotations from creative tourists about the emotions they felt while dancing during a flamenco class. First, Maya unambiguously reveals her enjoyment when she says that dancing flamenco in Seville 'is so nourishing when you're passionate about it like I am. It is wonderful. It's so nourishing that I feel myself living'. Second, in Celina's account below, enjoyment is revealed by the phrases 'I love it', 'I am grooving' and 'it's awesome':

> Well, I guess that personality wise I am pretty introvert and it's not that when I am dancing I go crazy or anything like that, but I feel things more acutely. I don't know how it comes out and how other people view it? But when I am enjoying like Andrés Peña's class, with the bulería, I LOVE IT! And, like I feel like I am – you know – I'm grooving [intonation of excitement] – you know – and it's awesome. And so I got that enjoyment thingy, I don't know, it's not something that I feel often normally in my daily life, but when I am dancing and when they're singing, it's like ... I don't know, it's hard to explain .... (p. 234)

What the words articulated by Celina also intimate is that her pleasurable experience is induced by the heightened bodily sensations she felt while engaging fully in the activity. Her account reveals the embodied and sentient character of the creative tourist experience, a point that we address in more details in Chapter 3.

Beyond the ubiquitous motives of novelty, pleasure, self-development (through learning) and relaxation, other less obvious motives were found to underlie creative tourist experiences. Matteucci's in-depth analysis of creative tourists' experiences of intangible heritage (flamenco dance and music) in Spain sheds some light on four additional motives. These are the need to remedy a lack of self-esteem, the need for self-exploration, the need to construct singular self-identities and the need for self-transformation. Table 2.2 summarises the motives underlying participation in creative tourism. In order to frame an understanding of the way people negotiate their identities and of the way people undergo transformative experiences, it is necessary to consider the role of the body in the creative tourist experience.

References

Aksenova, D., Cai, W., & Gebbels, M. (2022). Multi-sensory prosumption: How cooking classes shape perceptions of destinations. *International Journal of Contemporary Hospitality Management, 34*(9), 3417–3439. doi:10.1108/IJCHM-09-2021-1117

Amirou, R. (1995). *Imaginaire touristique et sociabilités du voyage*. Paris: Presses Universitaires de France.

Andrews, H. (2009). Tourism as a "moment of being". *Suomen Antropologi: Journal of the Finnish Anthropological Society, 34*(2), 5–21. doi:10.30676/jfas.116518

Argod, P. (2014). Art Visuel et médiation d'un tourisme créatif: de l'Expérience du voyage, de la pratique artistique et des "créatifs culturels". *Mondes du Tourisme, 10*, 47–61. doi:10.4000/tourisme.378

Aterianus-Owanga, A. (2019). 'KAAY FECC!' (Come Dance!): Economic, cultural and emotional flows in the "dance tourism" of *sabar* (Senegal-Europe). In M. Kaag, G. Khan-Mohammad, & S. Schmid (Eds.), *Destination Africa – Contemporary Africa as a centre of global encounter* (pp. 148–168). Leiden, The Netherlands: Brill.

Bachelard, G. (1943). *L'air et les songes*. Paris: Corti.

Bell, C. (2015). Tourists infiltrating authentic domestic space at Balinese home cooking schools. *Tourist Studies, 15*(1), 86–100. doi:10.1177/1468797614550958

Binkhorst, E. (2007). Creativity in tourism experiences: The case of Sitges. In G. Richards & J. Wilson (Eds.), *Tourism, creativity and development* (pp. 125–144). London: Routledge.

Bizas, E. (2014). *Learning Senegalese Sabar: Dancers and embodiment in New York and Dakar*. London: Berghahn Books.

Blapp, M., & Mitas, O. (2018). Creative tourism in Balinese rural communities. *Current Issues in Tourism, 21*(11), 1285–1311. doi:10.1080/13683500.2017.1358701

Bruner, E. (1986). Introduction: Experience and its expressions. In V. W. Turner & E. Bruner (Eds.), *The anthropology of experience* (pp. 3–30). Urbana, IL: University of Illinois Press.

Carvalho, M., Kastenholz, E., & Carneiro, M. J. (2021). Interaction as a central element of co-creative wine tourism experiences – Evidence from *Bairrada*, a Portuguese wine-producing region. *Sustainability, 13*, 9374. doi:10.3390/su13169374

Chang, L.-L. F., Backman, K., & Chih Huang, Y. (2014). Creative tourism: A preliminary examination of creative tourists' motivation, experience, perceived value and revisit intention. *International Journal of Culture, Tourism and Hospitality Research, 8*(4), 401–419. doi:10.1108/IJCTHR-04-2014-0032

Cohen, E. (1974). Who is a tourist? A conceptual classification. *Sociological Review, 22*, 527–555. doi:10.1111/j.1467-954X.1974.tb00507.x

Cohen, E. (1979). A phenomenology of tourist experiences. *Journal of the British Sociological Association, 13*(2), 179–201. doi:10.1177/003803857901300203

Creighton, M. R. (1995). Japanese craft tourism: Liberating the crane wife. *Annals of Tourism Research, 22*(2), 463–478. doi:10.1016/0160-7383(94)00086-7

Crompton, J. (1979). Motivations for pleasure vacation. *Annals of Tourism Research, 6*(4), 408–424. doi:10.1016/0160-7383(79)90004-5

Dann, G. M. S. (1977). Anomie, ego-enhancement and tourism. *Annals of Tourism Research, 4*, 184–194. doi:10.1016/0160-7383(77)90037-8

Dean, D., & Suhartanto, D. (2019). The formation of visitor behavioral intention to creative tourism: The role of push–pull motivation. *Asia Pacific Journal of Tourism Research, 24*(5), 393–403. doi:10.1080/10941665.2019.1572631

de Bruin, A., & Jelinčić, A. (2016). Toward extending creative tourism: Participatory experience tourism. *Tourism Review, 71*(1), 57–66. doi:10.1108/TR-05-2015-0018

Deleuze, G. (2002/1981). *Francis Bacon. La logique de la sensation*. Paris: Édition du Seuil.

Dias, A., González-Rodríguez, M. R., & Patuleia, M. (2021). Creative tourism destination competitiveness: An integrative model and agenda for future research. *Creative Industries Journal*. doi:10.1080/17510694.2021.1980672

Filep, S., Moyle, B. D., & Skavronskaya, L. (2022). Tourist wellbeing: Re-thinking hedonic and eudaimonic dimensions. *Journal of Hospitality & Tourism Research*. https://doi.org/10.1177/10963480221087964

Florida, R. (2002). *The rise of the creative class and how it's transforming work, leisure, community and everyday life*. New York, NY: Basic Books.

Gombault, A. (2014). Introduction au dossier: Pour un agenda de recherche sur le tourisme créatif en France. *Mondes du Tourisme, 10*, 2–5. doi:10.4000/tourisme.364

Gnoth, J., & Matteucci, X. (2014). A phenomenological view of the behavioral tourism research literature. *International Journal of Culture, Tourism and Hospitality Research, 8*(1), 3–21. doi:10.1108/IJCTHR-01-2014-0005

Graburn, N. H. H. (1989). Tourism: The sacred journey. In V. L. Smith (Ed.), *Hosts and guests*. Philadelphia, PA: University of Pennsylvania Press.

Gretzel, U., & Jamal, T. (2009). Conceptualizing the creative tourist class: Technology, mobility, and tourism experiences. *Tourism Analysis, 14*(4), 471–481. doi:10.3727/10 8354209X12596287114219

Hall, D., & Brown, F. (2006). *Tourism and welfare: Ethics, responsibility and sustained well-being*. Wallingford: CABI.

Hannam, K., & Knox, D. (2010). *Understanding tourism: A critical introduction*. London: Sage.

Hull, J. S., & Sassenberg, U. (2012). Creating new cultural visitor experiences on islands: Challenges and opportunities. *Journal of Tourism Consumption and Practice, 4*(2), 91–110.

Ilinčić, M. (2014). Benefits of creative tourism – The tourist perspective. In G. Richards & A. P. Russo (Eds.), *Alternative and creative tourism* (pp. 99–113). Arnhem: ATLAS.

Jelinčić, D. A., & Senkić, M. (2019). The value of experience in culture and tourism: The power of emotions. In G. Richards & N. Duxbury (Eds.), *A research agenda for creative tourism* (pp. 41–53). Cheltenham: Edward Elgar Publishing.

Jemielniak, D., & Przegalinska, A. (2020). *Collaborative society*. Boston, MA: MIT Press.

Jesus, D. S. V., Kamlot, D., & Dubeux, V. J. C. (2020). A critique of the creative economy, creative city and creative class from the global south. *International Journal of Business Administration, 11*(4), 1–12. doi:10.5430/ijba.v11n4p1

Kang, M., & Gretzel, U. (2012). Effects of podcast tours on tourism experiences in a national park. *Tourism Management, 33*(2), 440–455. doi:10.1016/j.tourman.2011.05.005

Khomsi, M. R., & Safaa, L. (2015). L'expérience au service de l'altérité: Marrakech à l'ère du tourisme créatif. In J.-M. Decroly (Ed.), *Le tourisme comme expérience: Regards interdisciplinaires sur le vécu touristique* (pp. 101–116). Montréal: Presses de l'Université du Québec.

Krätke, S. (2010). "Creative Cities" and the rise of the dealer class: A critique of Richard Florida's approach to urban theory. *International Journal of Urban and Regional Research, 34*(4), 835–853. doi:10.1111/j.1468-2427.2010.00939.x

Larsen, S. (2007). Aspects of a psychology of the tourist experience. *Scandinavian Journal of Hospitality and Tourism, 7*(1), 7–18. doi:10.1080/15022250701226014

Lash, S. (2006). Experience. *Theory, Culture & Society, 23*(2–3), 335–341. doi:10.1177/026327640602300262

MacCannell, D. (2013). *The tourist: A new theory of the leisure class*. Berkeley, CA: University of California Press.

Maddrell, A. (2011). 'Praying the Keeills'. Rhythm, meaning and experience on pilgrimage journeys in the Isle of Man. *Landabréfið – Journal of the Association of Icelandic Geographers, 25*, 15–29.

Marques, L. (2012). Boosting potential creative tourism resources: The case of Siby (Mali). *Journal of Tourism Consumption and Practice, 4*(2), 111–128.

Matteucci, X. (2012). *The tourist experience of intangible heritage: The case of flamenco consumers*. Unpublished Ph.D. thesis, Vienna University of Economics and Business (WU), Austria.

Matteucci, X. (2013). Experiencing flamenco: An examination of a spiritual journey. In S. Filep & P. Pearce (Eds.), *Tourist experience and fulfilment: Insights from positive psychology* (pp. 110–126). London: Routledge.

Matteucci, X. (2014). Forms of body usage in tourists' experiences of flamenco. *Annals of Tourism Research, 46*, 29–43. doi:10.1016/j.annals.2014.02.005

Matteucci, X. (2018a). Flamenco, tourists' experiences, and the meaningful life. In M. Uysal, J. Sirgy, & S. Kruger (Eds.), *Managing quality of life in tourism and hospitality* (pp. 10–23). Wallingford: CABI.

Matteucci, X. (2018b). Expériences touristiques, flamenco et hapax existentiel. *Leisure/Loisir, 42*(2), 185–204. doi:10.1080/14927713.2018.1449133

Matteucci, X. (2022). Existential hapax as tourist embodied transformation. *Tourism Recreation Research*, *47*(5–6), 631–635. doi:10.1080/02508281.2021.1934330

Matteucci, X., & Filep, S. (2017). Eudaimonic tourist experiences: The case of flamenco. *Leisure Studies*, *36*(1), 39–52. doi:10.1080/02614367.2015.1085590

McKercher, B. (2020). Cultural tourism market: A perspective paper. *Tourism Review*, *75*(1), 126–129. doi:10.1108/TR-03-2019-0096

Menet, J. (2020). *Entangled mobilities in the transnational salsa circuit: The Esperanto of the body, gender and ethnicity*. London: Routledge.

Mills, M. B. (2019). Authentic dishes, staged identities: Thailand's cooking schools for tourists. *Gastronomica*, *19*(2), 43–55. doi:10.1525/gfc.2019.19.2.43

Moscardo, G. (2009). Understanding tourist experience though mindfulness theory. In M. Kozak & A. Decrop (Eds.), *Handbook of tourist behavior, theory and practice* (pp. 99–115). London: Routledge.

Paschinger, E. (2021). Creative travellers in Austria. In N. Duxbury, S. Albino, & C. Pato de Carvalho (Eds.), *Creative tourism: Activating cultural resources and engaging creative travellers* (pp. 26–29). Wallingford: CAB International.

Pearce, P. L. (1982). *The social psychology of tourist behaviour*. Oxford: Pergamon.

Pearce, P. L. (2009). The relationship between positive psychology and tourist behaviour studies. *Tourism Analysis*, *14*, 37–48. doi:10.3727/108354209788970153

Pearce, P. L., Filep, S., & Ross, G. (2011). *Tourists, tourism and the good life*. London: Routledge.

Peterson, R. A. (1992). Understanding audience segmentation from elite and mass to omnivore and univore. *Poetics*, *21*(4), 243–258. doi:10.1016/0304-422X(92)90008-Q

Plog, S. C. (1987). Understanding psychographics in tourism research. In J. R. B. Ritchie & C. R. Goeldner (Eds.), *Travel, tourism, and hospitality research* (pp. 203–213). New York: Wiley.

Raymond, C. (2003). Case study – Creative tourism New Zealand: Creative tourism New Zealand and Australia council for the arts.

Raymond, C. (2007). Creative tourism New Zealand: The practical challenges of developing creative tourism. In G. Richards & J. Wilson (Eds.), *Tourism, creativity and development* (pp. 45–157). London: Routledge.

Remoaldo, P., Serra, J., Marujo, N., Alves, J., Gonçalves, A., Cabeça, S., & Duxbury, N. (2020). Profiling the participants in creative tourism activities: Case studies from small and medium sized cities and rural areas from Continental Portugal. *Tourism Management Perspectives*, *36*, 100746.

Richards, G. (2011). Creativity and tourism: The state of the art. *Annals of Tourism Research*, *38*(4), 1225–1253. doi:10.1016/j.annals.2011.07.008

Richards, G. (2020). Designing creative places: The role of creative tourism. *Annals of Tourism Research*, *85*, 102922. doi:10.1016/j.annals.2020.102922

Richards, G. (2021). *Re-thinking cultural tourism*. Cheltenham: Edward Elgar Publishing Ltd.

Richards, G., & Marques, L. (2018). *Creating synergies between cultural policy and tourism for permanent and temporary citizens*. Barcelona: UCLG.

Richards, G., & Wilson, J. (2006). Developing creativity in tourist experiences: A solution to the serial reproduction of culture? *Tourism Management*, *27*, 1209–1223. doi:10.1016/j.tourman.2005.06.002

Rigolot, F. (1992). *Journal de voyage de Michel de Montaigne*. Paris: Presses Universitaires de France.

Ross, D., & Saxena, G. (2019). Participative co-creation of archaeological heritage: Case insights on creative tourism in Alentejo, Portugal. *Annals of Tourism Research*, *79*, 102790. doi:10.1016/j.annals.2019.102790

Ryan, C. (2010). Ways of conceptualising the tourist experience: A review of literature. *Tourism Recreation Research*, *35*(1), 37–46. doi:10.1080/02508281.2010.11081617

Santayana, G. (1964). The philosophy of travel. *The Virginia Quarterly Review*, *40*(1), 1–10.

Saraniemi, S., & Kylänen, M. (2011). Problematizing the concept of tourism destination: An analysis of different theoretical approaches. *Journal of Travel Research, 50*(2), 133–143. doi:10.1177/0047287510362775

Saunders, R., Laing, J., & Weiler, B. (2013). Personal transformation through long-distance walking. In S. Filep & P. Pearce (Eds.), *Tourist experience and fulfillment: Insights from positive psychology* (pp. 127–146). London: Routledge.

Schmidt, C., & Little, D. E. (2007). Qualitative insights into leisure as a spiritual experience. *Journal of Leisure Research, 39*, 222–247. doi:10.1080/00222216.2007.11950106

Sharpley, R. (1994). *Tourism, tourists and society*. Huntingdon: ELM Publications.

Sharpley, R., & Sundaram, P. (2005). Tourism: A sacred journey? The case of Ashram tourism, India. *International Journal of Tourism Research, 7*, 161–171. doi:10.1002/jtr.522

Skinner, J. (2007). The salsa class: A complexity of globalization, cosmopolitans and emotions. *Identities: Global Studies in Culture and Power, 14*, 485–506. doi:10.1080/10702890701578480

Smith, M. K. (2016). *Issues in cultural tourism studies* (3rd ed.). London: Routledge.

Steiner, C. J., & Reisinger, Y. (2006). Understanding existential authenticity. *Annals of Tourism Research, 33*(2), 299–318. doi:10.1016/j.annals.2005.08.002

Suntikul, W., Agyeiwaah, E., Huang, W.-J., & Pratt, S. (2020). Investigating the tourism experience of Thai cooking classes: An application of Larsen's three-stage model. *Tourism Analysis, 25*(1), 107–122. doi:10.3727/108354220X15758301241684

Tan, S.-K., Kung, S.-F., & Luh, D.-B. (2013). A model of 'creative experience' in creative tourism. *Annals of Tourism Research, 41*, 153–174. doi:10.1016/j.annals.2012.12.002.

Tan, S.-K., Luh, D.-B., & Kung, S.-F. (2014). A taxonomy of creative tourists in creative tourism. *Tourism Management, 42*, 248–259. doi:10.1016/j.tourman.2013.11.008.

Toffler, A. (1980). *The third wave*. New York: Bantam Books.

Urbain, J.-D. (2007). Le touriste: Du sujet symptôme à l'homme qui rêve. *Synergies Pays Riverains de la Baltique, 4*, 15–25.

Uriely, N. (2005). The tourist experience: Conceptual developments. *Annals of Tourism Research, 32*(1), 199–216. doi:10.1016/j.annals.2004.07.008

Walter, P. (2017). Culinary tourism as living history: Staging, tourist performance and perceptions of authenticity in a Thai cooking school. *Journal of Heritage Tourism, 12*(4), 365–379. doi:10.1080/1743873X.2016.1207651

Wearing, S., Stevenson, D., & Young, T. (2010). *Tourist cultures: Identity, place and the traveller*. London: Sage.

Wearing, S., & Wearing, B. (2001). Conceptualizing the selves of tourism. *Leisure Studies, 20*, 143–159. doi:10.1080/02614360110051631

Willson, G. B., McIntosh, A. J, & Zahra, A. L. (2013). Tourism and spirituality: A phenomenological analysis. *Annals of Tourism Research, 42*, 150–168. doi:10.1016/j.annals.2013.01.016

Windress, K. (2016). Musical pilgrimages to Cuba: Negotiating tourism and musical learning in Cuban batá drumming. *MUSICultures, 43*(1), 132–152. Retrieved from https://journals.lib.unb.ca/index.php/MC/article/view/25263

Wurzburger, R., Aageson, T., Pattakos, A., & Pratt, S. (Eds.) (2010). *A Global conversation. How to provide unique creative experiences for travelers worldwide*. Santa Fe: Sunstone Press.

Zhang, Y., & Xie, P. F. (2019). Motivational determinates of creative tourism: A case study of Albergue art space in Macau. *Current Issues in Tourism, 22*(20), 2538–2549. doi:10.1080/13683500.2018.1517733

Zuluaga, D., & Guerra, D. (2021). A typology of creative travellers in Bogota, Colombia: The experience of 5Bogota. In N. Duxbury, S. Albino, & C. Pato de Carvalho (Eds.), *Creative tourism: Activating cultural resources and engaging creative travellers* (pp. 15–25). Wallingford: CAB International.

Chapter 3

Embodiment

> Our VAWAA (Vacation With An Artist) experience was fulfilling
> in every aspect. There is something about holding the brush in
> hand, with intention and focus, feeling the brush touch the paper,
> moving gracefully with each stroke. This act in my mind is sheer
> beauty. Now every time I see a piece of calligraphy, I picture the
> artist, moving, flowing and dancing with the characters. I'm glad
> we stopped to smell the Sumi ink.

As this introductory quotation from an American creative tourist of Japanese calligraphy in Kyoto intimates, tourists do not experience the world outside their bodies and senses. Earlier, a similar point was made by Veijola and Jokinen (1994) who asserted that the body provides a perceptual point of fixation between ourselves and the material world. Rather than *flâneurs* or passive consumers, creative tourists are active producers of their own experiences. Production entails practices and performances and all practices require a set of skills and a moving body in order to achieve certain goals and maximise satisfaction. Mertena, Kaaristo, and Edensor (2022) note that 'tourist practices mobilise embodied interactions with humans, non-humans and various materialities' (p. 1). Although tourists do not experience the world (including cultural heritage) beyond their bodies, creative tourism studies lack a critical analysis of tourist bodies, practices and performances. This neglect is not unique to creative tourism studies, as Hannam and Knox (2010) remark, tourism researchers have largely ignored 'the physical, social and cultural characteristics of human bodies and the experiences of living in, with and through such bodies' (p. 57). There are, however, some exceptions; one of them is the work by Palmer and Andrews (2020), which explores holistically the interrelated and inseparable relationship between the body, sense and lifeworld – described as an experience of 'sensuous dwelling' (p. 2).

The notion of embodiment relates to a complex process, which includes biological, sensorial, social and cultural dimensions. For example, Palmer and Andrews (2020) posit that the bodily being of a tourist is shaped by the coming together of culture and experience in different forms of tourism (e.g. heritage tourism, culinary tourism and adventure tourism). The body becomes the subject rather than the object of culture. Evringham, Obrador, and Tucker (2021) map a 20-year trajectory of theorising embodiment in tourism studies, focusing especially on the

The Creative Tourist: A Eudaimonic Perspective, 35–49
Copyright © 2024 by Xavier Matteucci and Melanie Kay Smith
Published under exclusive licence by Emerald Publishing Limited
doi:10.1108/978-1-83753-404-320241003

relationship between the senses and embodiment, described as 'relationalities of how sights, smells and sensations are central to the "tourist experience"' (p. 78). In addition to the five senses of sight, hearing, smell, taste and touch (visual, auditory, olfactory, gustatory and tactile) that provide information on the external environment (*exteroceptive senses*), Agapito, Mendes, and Valle (2013) also refer to sensory signals derived from the internal body pertaining to body awareness (*interoceptive senses*) and the interoceptive system, which includes the *proprioceptive* sense (*kinesthesia or* the sense of movement), the vestibular sense (balance), the visceral sense and the sense of *internal milieu* (e.g. pain and temperature).

Crouch (2000) has defined embodiment as 'the ways in which the individual grasps the world around her/him and makes sense of it in ways that engage both mind and body' (p. 63). Theories of embodiment are associated with the seminal work of the French philosopher Maurice Merleau-Ponty (1908–1961), and the later 'performative turn', which posits that 'tourism is about doing something accomplished through bodily involvement' (Prince, 2017, p. 2). Dwelling is another metaphor that has been used to understand the sensuous character of tourism (Crouch & Desforges, 2003; Farkić & Gebbels, 2022; Ingold, 2000; Palmer, 2018). Dwelling, Crouch, and Desforges (2003) note, entails the human actions, the practices and the unconscious knowledge that help us to navigate life situations, whether at home or on the move away from home.

Merleau-Ponty highlighted the central role of the body in the human experience. In *Phénoménologie de la Perception*, first published in 1945, Merleau-Ponty (2016) puts the body at the centre of the human experience, arguing that the body and the mind cannot be separated. By referring to the human being as 'un corps vécu' [a body-subject], Merleau-Ponty suggests that not only the body feels sensations but it also recognises them through the thought process in the mind. In the same vein, materialist philosopher Michel Onfray (1991) remarks that consciousness is not external to the body. In fact, consciousness is only one of the body's multiple modalities, it belongs to the body. The brain, Onfray notes, acts as a filter, which decodes sensual pleasure and gives pleasure its fullness and its intellectual form. Sensing is always situated in relation to other elements, such as various objects and both social and physical environments. Agapito et al. (2013) note that it is important to understand the sensory interrelationship between body, mind and environment. The experience of dancing, for instance, which belongs to the sensorial realm, is a function of various elements such as music, settings, objects (e.g. clothes, shoes and speakers), individuals (e.g. audience, partners and musicians) and the self (e.g. embodied experiences and fantasies). Referring to Saldanha's (2002) study in Goa, India, Edensor (2006) writes that

> beach raves are a complex amalgam of music, smells of sweat, kerosene and cannabis, the sight of the moon and coconut trees, the tactilities of moving bodies, sand and humidity, which combine – together with the varied effects of sensory enhancing drugs – to produce a subjective, intensely kinaesthetic experience. (p. 28)

Ruane (2017) also warns of the negative influences of mind-altering substances such as psychedelic drugs at so-called 'transformational festivals', including multi-sensory overload from noise, lights and spectacles, physical discomfort, sleep deprivation, exhaustion and disruption of emotional equilibrium. The inseparability of bodies from social and physical environments is clearly enunciated in Merleau-Ponty's (2016) work:

> The world is not what I think, but what I experience, I am open to the world, I undoubtedly communicate with it, but I do not possess it, it is inexhaustible. (Original in French below – translated by the authors)
>
> [Le monde est non pas ce que je pense, mais ce que je vis, je suis ouvert au monde, je communique indubitablement avec lui, mais je ne le possède pas, il est inépuisable]. (p. 17)

Because bodies feel and make sense of objects that have different shapes, colours, materiality and utility, Merleau-Ponty argues that perception is a creative process. 'Man is in the world, it is in the world that he knows himself' (p. 11). In other words, humans are not mere spectators of their lives; it is through bodily practices that they respond to situations, people and contingencies; it is, therefore, through bodily practices that tourists make sense of the world and negotiate their own embodied selves. Griffith (2021) similarly explains that embodied knowledge is how we understand the world, including sensations from the past as well as our continual engagement with the world through movement. She emphasises that by understanding the ways in which cognition is embodied, this allows us to pay attention to inner sensations that respond to both the natural and social external environment. Griffith (2021) also notes that bodies are never neutral, but are inscribed by experiences which are influenced by class, gender and race. Such influences affect how bodies are read, received and understood by ourselves and others.

Such philosophical stances towards the body and perception resonate with the view of American pragmatists, William James and John Dewey, who argue that human agency 'is always a series of bodily activities immersed in the ongoing flow of organism-environment interactions that constitutes experience' (Johnson & Rohrer, 2007, p. 22). In their ethnographic study with circus artists in Montréal (Québec), Richard, Glaveanu, and Aubertin (2022) provide some insights into the emergence of embodied creative ideas through the interplay of multiple elements. It has become common for circus artists to run workshops, which engage participants bodily in their creative practices and not only as spectators. Circus has become more and more multidisciplinary and hybrid, now involving theatre, music, storytelling, dance, arts and technology, a combination of movement, emotions and social interactions (Richard et al., 2022). The latter authors observe how a social life event, such as the yellow vest protest in France, can prompt creative ideas through bodily movement:

> [...] reading in the news about the yellow vest protest in France, a French artist expressed the desire to explore, through movement, what the color yellow meant for her. This desire unfolded into

> meaningful discussions between the artist and the teacher estab-
> lishing an open and collaborative internal climate. This climate
> supported a rich explorative journey heading in widely varied
> directions. From moving with various yellow props, performing
> through yellow pieces of clothing on the floor, to expressing "yel-
> low" emotions through the body, the political attachment of the
> artist to her country set the stage for embodied ideation. (p. 8)

William James, John Dewey and Maurice Merleau-Ponty paved the way towards a materialist philosophy of the body. In Deleuzian philosophy, the human experience cannot be understood outside the body because the body is the form through which consciousness emerges (Onfray, 1991). The Deleuzian body is unbounded in that it is in a perpetual process of transformation; it is affected by and affecting other subjects and objects. Deleuze uses the term 'becoming' rather than 'being' to refer to the constant process of human experiencing the world; in fact, Deleuze, with his collaborator Guattari (1980), metaphorically compares the process of becoming to 'un voyage immobile' (a stationary journey) (p. 244). The notion of movement and the modes of propagation are central to the idea of becoming, which is useful for grasping the relational processes of re-arrangement of the self through travel. What is not visible and easy to unearth is the tem-poral dynamic involved in tourist practices. What we mean is that every tourist action performed and every emotion felt may be transitory; yet, these practices and emotions are the culminating assemblage of a person's history. For instance, because individuals are not born with a set of skills (Ingold, 1996), to situate and understand creative tourists' experiences, attention should be given to tourists' life trajectories, that is, to the tourists' socio-cultural contexts within which past and new skills are acquired. In a similar vein, some authors have argued that 'emplacement' advances embodiment theory, as it takes into consideration the relationship between mind, body, place, social construction and meaning within a moving world. In other words, the concept of emplacement reveals human agency as situated or emplaced, which entails movements as well as a fully sensuous par-ticipative body. Emplacement may be applicable to physical activities like sport that involve moving through sensorial environments (Bäckström, 2014) as well as in cultural performative events like bullfights (Pink, 2011).

3.1 Creative Tourist Embodied Experiences

Many commentators recognise the pedagogical potential of embodied practice and collaborative experience design process for creative tourism (e.g. Duxbury & Bakas, 2021; Duxbury & Richards, 2019; Miettinen, Erkkilä-Hill, Koistinen, Jokela, & Hiltunen, 2019); yet, surprisingly, research on embodied experiences and creativity is rather scarce within the field of creative tourism. In the work that has scrutinised the role of the body and senses in the creative tourist experience, we can identify two main areas of attention. On the one hand, from a management perspective, creative tourist experiences have been linked to co-creation and the memorability of sensory experiences. Yin, Huang, and Wang (2023) describe how memory is closely related to tourists' embodied participation in cultural creative tourism, environment perception and meaning cognition. Their findings highlight the importance of what they call 'embodied engagement', which is composed of sensory participation and environmental atmosphere. This might include tasting food and appreciating architecture as well as physically participating in tourism activities such as making artwork. This is especially true of embodied experiences of cities, as researched by Satama and Räikkönen (2020) in which they explore collective memories through narrations of multi-sensory encounters, including cultural, creative and social elements. Agapito et al. (2013) highlight the need for a holistic approach to *sensescapes*, for example, *soundscapes*, *tastescapes*, *haptiscapes* and *smellscapes*. Skyros (2023), one of the oldest and most famous agencies offering holistic retreats, highlights perfectly the relationship between external and internal landscapes in its promotion of art holidays:

> Inspired by the breathing of the pine trees, the whispers of the nocturnal sea or the memories of rocks blessed with the wisdom of so many generations, people embark on a serene, inspirational journey that takes them beyond the boundaries of their imagination. The beautiful images they create, with help from our facilitators, through their unexplored inner landscapes make them proud of a creativity some never suspected they possess!

On the other hand, from a socio-psychological perspective, creative tourists' practices and embodied experiences have been associated with well-being outcomes. For instance, Skyros (2023) presents their 'Curative Writing' courses as

> a series of unique practices designed to take us beneath the noisy mind to that quiet, endlessly creative place within that is always available to us ... writing is good for us: it calms the anxious mind, it finds meaning when a personal or global narrative might seem senseless, it restores the balance of inner and outer.

In the following two sections, firstly, we attend to some of this work on creative tourist bodies, practices and performances using the example of and research on flamenco. Secondly, we consider the link between embodied experiences and learning.

3.1.1 Creative Tourists' Forms of Body Usage

What the work of Matteucci (2014) has revealed is that beyond mere educational needs, creative tourists engage in artistic activities like dance and music in order to fulfil some unconscious needs, which can be linked to different forms of body usage that are deployed simultaneously. Matteucci notes that flamenco tourists use their bodies towards different ends. The first form of body usage is linked to disciplined bodily practices that are sought after by the creative tourists in order to remedy a lack of self-esteem. The second form of body usage fulfils the need for self-expression and exploration. The third form reveals tourists' artistic practices as a means to achieve social status and a way to resist social norms.

Firstly, through intensive practice and disciplined lifestyle during their stay in Seville, the creative tourists regiment their bodies as a way to enhance their self-esteem. The female flamenco dancers were found to be particularly concerned with making their bodies more feminine. In order to unearth some of the women's concern with their self-appearance, Matteucci notes that one needs to attend to tourists' imaginations, fantasies and to the meanings creative tourists ascribe to the stereotypical image of the female flamenco dancer, which tourists describe as sensual and seductive. For instance, one creative tourist said about Alicia Márquez, her Andalusian dance instructor and a well-known flamenco artist, that she 'has the style that is very feminine. And for me as a woman [it] is very important' (p. 35). To further illustrate this concern with body image, the following excerpt from another creative tourist reveals the close connection between flamenco movements and the social construct of femininity:

> In fact, I see my handwork as a strength, like 'I've been working hard on my hands [laugh], so … well I think that's something inevitable. For example, not to have the greatest foot technique to mark the compás (rhythmic cycles) is [ok], but for me the handwork is … because hands have all the stylishness and the finesse like … Well, yeah, I mean the trunk, the strength and all that, but the hands – it's the tip that gives a bit of gentleness and grace. (p. 35)

For many female creative tourists, the flamenco practice enabled them to embrace their feminine side. Fig. 3.1 illustrates the gendered space of flamenco class and the link between flamenco and femininity. Before joining flamenco dance classes in Seville, Jil, a 31-year-old French woman, admitted not regarding her body as desirable, yet, towards the end of her stay in Seville, her body image had changed. Overall, the creative experience had been empowering. By associating the woman body with the flamenco dance, Matteucci argues, 'a form of femininity is celebrated, whereby gendered identities are created' (p. 35). Beyond a concern with body image, the creative tourist is often confronted with activities that require a set of skills that they may not possess. In light of challenging situations, and in order to acquire some skills, dedication and discipline are needed if tourists want to achieve their educational goals. In creative embodied experiences of dance, and the performing arts more generally, efforts, physical pain (e.g. bruised feet) and discomfort often constitute the necessary conditions for optimal development.

Secondly, creative tourist bodies are unveiled as sites for expression and exploration. Drawing from Featherstone (2010), Matteucci suggests that '[u]nlike the disciplined body, which depends on a particular body image, the expressive body is a "body without a clearly defined image" [.] The expressive body is an affective body, which relies on the body's sensory functions' (p. 36). Through performances, tourists deploy their creative potential in an attempt at embodying a variety of

Fig. 3.1.   Women Practicing Flamenco in Andalusia (Author: Mido Arts).

flamenco feelings (e.g. love, joy, anger, pain and sorrow). We have already seen that, sometimes, this sensual exploration leads tourists to discover and accept their feminine side. However, this exploration may also help them to fulfil their aesthetic needs, which, in turn, may produce self-transformative experiences. The quote below illustrates the intensities of the emotions felt during the dance classes, which reveals the creative embodied tourist experience of flamenco as a powerful source of learning and understanding:

> Physically, I've discovered sensations that I didn't know before. I've learned that I could do certain things with my body that not even [I had thought I could do before]… It's like when you see someone dancing Capoeira – I'm like 'wow'! It's amazing! Well, when you manage to do it with your own body, you… So, physically, I've discovered amazing sensations. (Matteucci, 2017, p. 58)

Likewise, below, Ebony articulates how she has discovered herself through her embodied experience of the flamenco feelings:

> You can express yourself in so many ways with flamenco. Yeah, so I guess that's my experience here, it's helping me touch part of myself that ... [laugh] It's helping me get in touch with parts of myself that I didn't know .... (Matteucci, 2012, p. 168)

As a site of exploration, the body is a permeable space in which the creative tourist moves, feels, experiences awe and eventually becomes something else (Matteucci, 2014). In Chapter 5 of this book, we will return to the transformative dimension of creative tourism, highlighting the links between embodied experiences, finding inspiration and feelings of well-being.

Thirdly, the body is linked to taste and desires and is therefore associated with consumptive practices. Creative flamenco tourists buy products that give them a sense of identity and belongingness. Paradoxically, while stereotypical images of flamenco performers may shape the way creative tourists consume flamenco, these aficionados show a desire to differentiate themselves from other social bodies. Thus, by consuming a range of flamenco-related products such as flamenco guitars, shoes and dance accessories, creative tourists' practices are viewed as a means to achieve a distinctive social status. Referring to the work of Paechter (2006), Matteucci (2014) argues that '[e]mbodying the flamenco look is seen as a central element which legitimises participation in the flamenco community of practice' (p. 41). Moreover, beyond the pursuit of status, women by choosing flamenco dance and men choosing flamenco guitar, Matteucci notes that creative tourists' practices contribute to the reinforcement of social and gender roles. In addition, through unconventional tourist practices such as flamenco dance and music, creative tourist bodies are described as spaces where existential experiences are sought, spaces where established social structures and conventions are challenged. In opposition to mainstream cultural tourists who may experience flamenco as a fun, trivial activity during their holiday, the creative flamenco tourists see their serious flamenco practice as authentic and marginal. This recalls the work of Stebbins (1996) on so-called *serious leisure* and his application of this theory to cultural tourism. This also reminds us of MacCannell's (1976) analysis of back regions, whereby some more educated tourists look for opportunities to explore a locale beyond the glossy representations of the tourism industry. This suggests that creative tourists believe that they can distinguish between authentic cultural experiences from commodified experiences. In short, the creative tourists' practices and performances are deemed to correspond to a quest for embodying their marginal selves; a point that we address later in this book.

3.1.2 Embodied Learning Experiences

In the creative tourist experience, tourists' intimate entanglement with other bodies, materialities and non-materialities (e.g. music) may also mobilise fantasies and foster learning. Research on tourist dance performances has contributed to shedding some light on how tourists can learn through their bodies. Aterianus-Owanga's (2019) ethnographic work on sabar in Senegal indicates that the experience of dance tourism in Africa is closely connected to various social and identity transformations. Even though the majority of the dance tourists are white, European women, their experiences bring them closer to African culture and way of life. Indeed, Palmer and Andrews (2020) illustrate how 'bodies inform outsiders of the beliefs, rituals and cultural practices of that particular society' (p. 29). In an anthropological sense, tourist bodies learn how to behave in a different cultural context. The women also participate in a journey of self-development and self-construction. The kinaesthetic experience of dancing sabar is described as being inexplicably addictive, irresistible, allowing the women to feel more self-confident, healed, even to discover 'the real truth inside'. In a similar fashion, the holistic retreat Cortijo Romero (2023) promotes the benefits of a week spent learning tango by claiming that

> [t]ango strengthens skills such as body awareness, empathy, trust, patience, and connection with others. It is meditative and calming, absorbing and restorative. It is proven to stimulate, and create new neural pathways.

McClure (2014) undertook research at international salsa congresses including numerous interviews and observations of participants. This work examines the way in which social salsa dancing opens up capacities for participants to make sense of themselves and others by 'being-a-body-with-other-bodies' through interactions and momentary connections (p. 113). This involves, for example, paying attention to and adapting to different dance partners. The three kinds of senses and skills that he identifies with learning salsa are related to one's bodily movements, contact with a partner and listening to the music. McClure argues that practice of social dancing encourages proprioceptive and kinaesthetic values to emerge; dancers experience a highly intersubjective form of embodiment involving both joy and the potential for self-discovery and emancipation. The potential of dance for the discovery of new bodily sensations was clearly articulated by some flamenco dance tourists in Matteucci's (2017) study. While female dancers often found it difficult to verbalise their bodily feelings, their accounts intimate moving bodies as entangled machines of knowledge production. Not only female dancers felt that they had acquired new motor skills and had become aware of what their body could do, but they also experienced highly pleasurable sensations. Likewise, McClure (2014) reports how practitioners of bodily practices like yoga, pilates, forms of martial arts and some sports have for many centuries described the positive, pleasurable and transformative effects of developing enhanced somatic awareness. Ravn (2022) discusses both sports and more creative practices like dance, arguing that under certain conditions, embodied abilities like running or mountain biking can enhance both physical and mental skills, especially when it comes to performance and competition. Dance, on the other hand, is more connected to the degree of expression when making certain movements or sequences of movements.

Ravn (2022) compares improvised forms of dance with those that involve genre-based skills (e.g. flamenco and Irish step dancing). She argues that improvisers tend to engage in spontaneous 'letting things happen' (p. 6). Nevertheless, in many improvised dance forms (e.g. Argentinian tango), practitioners are expected to have trained and developed certain skills before they can participate. It is important to note that many creative dance tourists would lack the specialised skills to be able to improvise. Indeed, both McClure (2014) and Aterianus-Owanga (2019) differentiate between beginners and more experienced dance tourists. McClure finds that in salsa dancing, beginners focus more on bodily or kinaesthetic awareness (e.g. basic movements and learning steps), whereas more advanced dancers value musicality and developing a more refined tactile connection with a partner. Aterianus-Owanga (2019) shows how the meaning of sabar-related dance tourism changes over time depending on levels of experience and frequency of visits. This can affect expectations, including preferences for more traditional or more modern dance styles. Matteucci (2012) similarly observes that the more earnest flamenco aficionados, who stay longer in Spain than the more casual flamenco learners, tend to report greater motivation to learn advanced techniques from local artists. However, some creative dance courses sidestep the need for prior experience; for instance, Skyros (2023) offers so-called Freedom-DANCE, which involves:

> Freedom to move your body without learned steps or routine; freedom to let go of comparisons, judgments and criticisms; freedom to be yourself and connect with others... We let our dance develop and transform, releasing old patterns and finding new ways to move and relate to ourselves and others.

There may be other forms of creative practice in addition to dance, such as music or theatre in which the performer or participant is constantly required to renegotiate individuality and collectivity in response to others in a process of co-creativity (Griffith, 2021). Skyros (2023), for example, describes the emotional individual and group experience during its 'Singing & Music' courses: 'expect to laugh a lot and cry sometimes. Most of all expect to connect with your own heart and bond with a wonderful group of people. This is about inner and outer performance' and 'when we sing together and engage in creativity we naturally promote happiness, health, and harmony in ourselves and in the world we live in'.

Through variegated practices and performances, creative tourists have the opportunity to sensually experience and immerse themselves in unfamiliar environments. By environment, we understand both the social and the material spatial conditions that afford multiple opportunities for tourist creativity to emerge and grow. The seminal works of the American psychologist James Jerome Gibson (1904–1979) provided an initial understanding of the senses as active and interrelated rather than passive and mutually exclusive. In line with Gibson's (1966) observation of the complex, multi-sensuality of human perception, Agapito et al. (2013) maintain that in the overall tourist experience, no single sense seems to dominate constantly. Some examples of multi-sensory experiences can also be taken from creative forms of gastronomic tourism. For instance, in a cooking class in Thailand, creative tourists can feel the textures of ingredients and utensils, smell and taste spices and exotic fruits and listen to the rich sounds and voices within heterogenous street markets and within the bounded space of kitchens. Aksenova, Cai, and Gebbels (2022) argue that

> [w]hat differentiates a cooking class from other culinary experiences is the prosuming multisensory process. Instead of consuming the final products through dining, the sensations intertwine and evolve through the prosuming process of cooking, which is complex, dynamic and memorable. (p. 3432)

This sensual and performative immersion allows creative tourists to understand local cultural customs and practices. In the case of cooking classes of national dishes of the Republic of Tatarstan, Russia, immersive and embodied experiences serve as a conduit through which creative visitors could deepen their knowledge and understanding of Tatarstan's culture and traditions (Aksenova et al., 2022). Likewise, in the context of cooking schools in Thailand, Walter (2017) observes that while cooking with their hosts, tourists 'learned through their noses, mouths, hands, eyes and ears' (p. 376).

The creative tourist body, whether auditory, gustatory, haptic, olfactory, visual or kinaesthetic is, therefore, a powerful facilitator of learning. Some olfactory experiences, for instance, are constituent of self-knowledge processes. Matteucci (2017) has documented the olfactory experience of an American music tourist in Seville who became aware of his own cultural sensitivity towards unpleasant smells such as horse manure. Through shared practices and through new modes of being and doing, not only creative tourists learn about themselves, the local people and the local culture, but also a personal bond with the destination is established.

The literature on creative tourism suggests that there is a link between rich multi-sensory experiences and a close connection with hosts and the region visited. For instance, in her study of tourists' experiences at home-cooking schools in Bali, Bell (2015) notes that by cooking and eating in the domestic environment of local Balinese people, tourists' senses are not only highly stimulated, but their perception of place is also greatly enhanced. In line with the dwelling perspective articulated by Ingold (2000), the sensuous tourist encounter with places and people facilitates, as Crouch (1999) puts it, a lay geographical knowledge. Tourists' sensuous practices such as whisking fish sauce, soy sauce and sugar in a bowl or stir-frying shallots and garlic constitute modes of appropriation of Balinese cultural practices, which are constituent of tourists' sense of place and knowledge, and which mobilise tourists' skills and fantasies. Lay geographical knowledge is thus a learning process always in the making both through sensual engagement in situ and shaped by the influence of representations.

In addition, Kim and Lehto (2013) have argued that through the co-creation of cultural activities, such as cooking classes, visitors are able to challenge stereotypes, myths and taken-for-granted ideas towards places, which are constituted through mainstream media discourse and marketing. In Cuba, Windress (2016) observes that in batá drumming experiences through informal networks, Western tourists not only develop a cultural understanding and empathy for indigenous people but also genuine friendships between them and Cubans can be established. By way of further illustration, in a study conducted by Carvalho, Kastenholz, and Carneiro (2021) in Bairrada, a wine region of Portugal, personal bonds with places and its people could be forged through harvesting experiences. In this study, a 32-year-old woman reflects on her harvesting experience in the following terms:

> The moment I was there ... it's something that isn't that fast [...] it's a personal experience that is real ... and the difference is the fact that you are experiencing an ancient tradition [...] and suddenly you see yourself being part of the wine production process, not from a touristic perspective but like the locals do, working beside them. For me, it was a reflexive moment. (p. 11)

Carvalho et al. (2021) stress the central role of the tourists' immersion in the vineyards landscape (or taskscape) and the tourists' active role in picking grapes together with local women and men in shaping tourists' sense of place as well as their sense of being in their own bodies. The encounters between tourists and local harvesters are more than merely transactional and ephemeral; they are defined by the ways local harvesters carry out their tasks and live their lives in their home region. Anchored in a peculiar territory, harvesting practices are endowed with a rich history as these have been crafted, refined and perfected over time. The creative tourist's sense of place is, therefore, constituted through the enactment of culturally rich, embedded practices and materialities of the host region (Franklin, 2003). This argument about tourist learning through place-specific cultural practices is also evidenced in tourism promotion. For instance, Indigenous Tourism BC (2023) in Canada organises cultural and creative tourism experiences and describes how 'art and artefacts are alive in Indigenous culture – embodied and expressed by the living people, who carry the knowledge of their ancestors and share it with you'. They invite tourists to engage in 'lively interaction' with indigenous culture, including traditional craft and storytelling. As a consequence of mingling with participants, narratives of developing friendships with locals and fellow tourists are not uncommon in creative tourists' experiences; the development of relationships is a point that we will turn to in the following chapter.

References

Agapito, D., Mendes, J., & Valle, P. (2013). Conceptualizing the sensory dimension of tourist experiences. *Journal of Destination Marketing & Management, 2*(2), 62–73. doi:10.1016/j.jdmm.2013.03.001

Aksenova, D., Cai, W., & Gebbels, M. (2022). Multi-sensory prosumption: How cooking classes shape perceptions of destinations. *International Journal of Contemporary Hospitality Management, 34*(9), 3417–3439. doi:10.1108/IJCHM-09-2021-1117

Aterianus-Owanga, A. (2019). "KAAY FECC!" (Come Dance!): Economic, cultural and emotional flows in the "dance tourism" of *sabar* (Senegal-Europe). In M. Kaag, G. Khan-Mohammad, & S. Schmid (Eds.), *Destination Africa – Contemporary Africa as a centre of global encounter* (pp. 148–168). Leiden: Brill.

Bäckström, Å. (2014). Knowing and teaching kinaesthetic experience in skateboarding: An example of sensory emplacement. *Sport, Education and Society*, *19*(6), 752–772. doi:10.1080/13573322.2012.713861

Bell, C. (2015). Tourists infiltrating authentic domestic space at Balinese home cooking schools. *Tourist Studies*, *15*(1), 86–100. doi:10.1177/1468797614550958

Carvalho, M., Kastenholz, E., & Carneiro, M. J. (2021). Interaction as a central element of co-creative wine tourism experiences – Evidence from *Bairrada*, a Portuguese wine-producing region. *Sustainability*, *13*, 9374. doi:10.3390/su13169374

Crouch, D. (Ed.). (1999). *Leisure/tourism geographies*. London: Routledge.

Crouch, D. (2000). Places around us: Embodied lay geographies in leisure and tourism. *Leisure Studies*, *19*(2), 63–76. doi:10.1080/026143600374752

Crouch, D., & Desforges, L. (2003). The sensuous in the tourist encounter: Introduction: The power of the body in tourist studies. *Tourist Studies*, *3*(1), 5–22. doi:10.1177/1468797603040528

Deleuze, G., & Guattari, F. (1980). *Capitalisme et Schizophrénie 2: Mille plateaux*. Paris: Les Éditions de Minuits.

Duxbury, N., & Bakas, F. E. (2021). Creative tourism: A humanistic paradigm in practice. In M. Della Lucia & E. Giudici (Eds.), *Humanistic management and sustainable tourism: Human, social and environmental challenges* (pp. 111–131). London: Routledge.

Duxbury, N., & Richards, G. (2019). Towards a research agenda for creative tourism: Developments, diversity, and dynamics. In N. Duxbury & G. Richards (Eds.), *A research agenda for creative tourism* (pp. 1–14). Cheltenham, UK: Edward Elgar Publishing.

Edensor, T. (2006). Sensing tourist spaces. In C. Minca & T. Oakes (Eds.), *Travels in paradox: Remapping tourism* (pp. 23–46), London: Rowman and Littlefield.

Evringham, P., Obrador, P., & Tucker, H. (2021). Trajectories of embodiment in *Tourist Studies*. *Tourist Studies*, *21*(1), 70–83. doi:10.1177/1468797621990300

Farkić, J., & Gebbels, M. (2022). *The adventure tourist: Being, knowing, becoming*. Bingley: Emerald Publishing.

Featherstone, M. (2010). Body, image and affect in consumer culture. *Body & Society*, *16*(1), 193–221. doi:10.1177/1357034X09354357

Franklin, A. (2003). *Tourism: An introduction*. London: Sage.

Gibson, J. J. (1966). *The senses considered as perceptual systems*. Boston, MA: Houghton Mifflin.

Griffith, A. (2021). Embodied creativity in the fine and performing arts. *Journal of Creativity*, *31*, 100010. doi:10.1016/j.yjoc.2021.100010

Hannam, K., & Knox, D. (2010). *Understanding tourism: A critical introduction*. London: Sage.

Indigenous Tourism BC. (2023). Arts & culture. Retrieved from https://www.indigenousbc.com/things-to-do/arts-and-culture

Ingold, T. (1996). Situating action V: The history and evolution of bodily skills. *Ecological Psychology*, *8*(2), 171–182. doi:10.1207/s15326969eco0802_5

Ingold, T. (2000). *The perception of the environment: Essays in livelihood, dwelling and skill*. London: Routledge.

Johnson, M., & Rohrer, T. (2007). We are live creatures: Embodiment, American pragmatism, and the cognitive organism. In J. Zlatev, T. Ziemke, F. Roz, & R. Driven (Eds.), *Body, language, and mind* (pp. 17–54). Berlin: Mouton de Gruyter.

Kim, S., & Lehto, X. Y. (2013). Projected and perceived destination brand personalities: The case of South Korea. *Journal of Travel Research*, *52*(1), 117–130. doi:10.1177/0047287512457259

MacCannell, D. (1976). *The tourist: A new theory of the leisure class.* New York, NY: Schocken.

Matteucci, X. (2012). *The tourist experience of intangible heritage: The case of flamenco consumers.* Ph.D. thesis, Vienna University of Economics and Business (WU), Vienna.

Matteucci, X. (2014). Forms of body usage in tourists' experiences of flamenco. *Annals of Tourism Research, 46,* 29–43. doi:10.1016/j.annals.2014.02.005

Matteucci, X. (2017). Tourists' accounts of learning and positive emotions through sensory experiences. In S. Filep, J. Laing, & M. Csikszentmihalyi (Eds.), *Positive tourism* (pp. 54–67), London: Routledge.

McClure, B. (2014). "Endless possibilities": Embodied experiences and connections in social salsa dancing. *PhoenEx, 9*(2) (fall/winter), 112–135. doi:10.22329/p.v9i2.4026

Merleau-Ponty, M. (2016). *Phénoménologie de la perception.* Paris: Gallimard.

Mertena, I., Kaaristo, M., & Edensor, T. (2022). Tourist skills. *Annals of Tourism Research, 94,* 103387. doi:10.1016/j.annals.2022.103387

Miettinen, S., Erkkilä-Hill, J., Koistinen, S., Jokela, T., & Hiltunen, M. (2019). Stories of design, snow, and silence: Creative tourism landscape in Lapland. In N. Duxbury & G. Richards (Eds.), *A research agenda for creative tourism* (pp. 69–83). Cheltenham: Edward Elgar Publishing.

Onfray, M. (1991). *L'Art de jouir. Pour un matérialisme hédoniste.* Paris: Grasset.

Paechter, C. (2006). Power, knowledge, and embodiment in communities of sex/gender practice. *Women's Studies International Forum, 29*(1), 13–26. doi:10.1016/j.wsif.2005.10.003

Palmer, C. (2018). *Being and dwelling through tourism: An anthropological perspective.* Abingdon: Routledge.

Palmer, C., & Andrews, H. (2020). Tourism and embodiment: Animating the field. In C. Palmer & H. Andrews (Eds.), *Tourism and embodiment* (pp. 1–8). Abingdon: Routledge.

Pink, S. (2011). From embodiment to emplacement: Re-thinking competing bodies, senses and spatialities. *Sport, Education and Society, 16*(3), 343–355. doi:10.1080/13573322.2011.565965

Prince, S. (2017). Dwelling in the tourist landscape: Embodiment and everyday life among the craft-artists of Bornholm. *Tourist Studies, 18*(1), 63–82. doi:10.1177/1468797617710598

Ravn, S. (2022). Embodied learning in physical activity: Developing skills and attunement to interaction. *Front Sports Act Living, 31*(4), 795733. doi:10.3389/fspor.2022.795733

Richard, V., Glaveanu, V., & Aubertin, P. (2022). The embodied journey of an idea: An exploration of movement creativity in circus arts. *Journal of Creative Behavior, 57*(2), 221–236. doi:10.1002/jocb.571

Romero, C. (2023). Arts, creativity & expression. Retrieved from https://www.cortijo-romero.co.uk

Ruane, D. (2017). "Wearing down of the self": Embodiment, writing and disruptions of identity in transformational festival fieldwork. *Methodological Innovations, 10*(1), 1–11. doi:10.1177/2059799117720611

Saldanha, A. (2002). Music tourism and factions of bodies in Goa. *Tourist Studies, 2*(1), 43–62. doi:10.1177/1468797602002001096

Satama, S., & Räikkönen, J. (2020). Exploring the embodied narrations of the city. *International Journal of Culture, Tourism and Hospitality Research, 14*(3), 373–383. doi:10.1108/IJCTHR-10-2019-0180

Skyros. (2023). Retrieved from https://www.skyros.com

Stebbins, R. A. (1996). Cultural tourism as serious leisure. *Annals of Tourism Research, 23*(4), 948–950. doi:10.1016/0160-7383(96)00028-X

Veijola, S., & Jokinen, E. (1994). The body in tourism. *Theory, Culture and Society, 11*(3), 125–151. doi:10.1177/026327694011003006

Walter, P. (2017). Culinary tourism as living history: Staging, tourist performance and perceptions of authenticity in a Thai cooking school. *Journal of Heritage Tourism*, *12*(4), 365–379. doi:10.1080/1743873X.2016.1207651

Windress, K. (2016). Musical pilgrimages to Cuba: Negotiating tourism and musical learning in Cuban Batá Drumming. *MUSICultures*, *43*(1), 132–152. Retrieved from https://journals.lib.unb.ca/index.php/MC/article/view/25263

Yin, Z., Huang, A., & Wang, J. (2023). Memorable tourism experiences' formation mechanism in cultural creative tourism: From the perspective of embodied cognition. *Sustainability*, *15*, 4055. doi:10.3390/su15054055

Chapter 4

Creative Tourist Spaces

Our discussion of embodied experiences in the previous chapter alluded to the central role of space in tourism. In fact, Wearing et al. (2010) remind us that '[t]ourism is first and foremost about space' (p. 76). It would seem amiss to study the creative tourist experience without considering tourists' interactions with space and place. Before people leave home to become tourists, they often project themselves to foreign places and fantasise about exotic sights, people, food and other materialities that they may encounter in distant locales. This observation brings us to consider *tourist space* as a multidimensional concept. While we may be tempted to associate space with physical settings such as buildings, streets, city squares, local cafés, resorts, geographical areas and wildlife habitats, Crouch, Aronsson, and Wahlström (2001) invite us to think of space as both a material context and an imaginative realm that is constructed in the mind. This imaginative space emerges through past travel experiences and destination images, which emanate from a vast range of commercial and non-commercial information sources. Amirou (1995) contributes to this discussion by suggesting that, in fact, the tourist experience is largely instilled with expectations, fantasies and myths that originate from the tourist's culture. An example of such myths is the romanticised image of the Spanish gypsy woman in the Western imaginary. Caltabiano (2009) explains that the Western fascination with the exotic gypsy was born in the late eighteenth century when 'the French and Italians created the myth of the dark mysterious and sexual gypsy woman' (p. 14). Bizet's famous opera *Carmen* exemplifies this myth. Amirou (1994) goes so far as to argue that the tourist imaginary is, in fact, *une illusion touristique*. It is deemed an illusion in that Western tourists have become fascinated not by reality itself but by a world of fanciful images that people take as real, or in other words, as Boorstin (1964) put it, the tourist 'has come to expect both more strangeness and more familiarity than the world naturally offers' (p. 79). The notion of tourist space, therefore, is endowed with both a tangible and an intangible dimension. Not only do both dimensions conflict with each other but they also both cohabit within the self, thus sometimes leaving tourists confused about the meanings and authenticity of the cultural space they are exposed to. In this regard, in his Thailand-based study, Walter (2017) notes that, infused by the Western ideas of a mythical Thai past, creative culinary tourists encounter a rather equivocal space of Thai everyday life

The Creative Tourist: A Eudaimonic Perspective, 51–67
Copyright © 2024 by Xavier Matteucci and Melanie Kay Smith
Published under exclusive licence by Emerald Publishing Limited
doi:10.1108/978-1-83753-404-320241004

and culture. Space, therefore, as Crouch et al. (2001) contend, acts as 'a medium through which the tourist negotiates her or his world, tourism signs and contexts, and may construct her or his own distinctive meanings' (p. 254).

Rarely the tourist is isolated from other humans in tourism contexts; hence, tourist settings are primarily shared spaces. This observation calls for attending to the kinds of socialities that emerge from interactions within tourist spaces. Drawing from Grosz (1995), Wearing and Wearing (1996) have argued for a feminist conceptualisation of the tourist space as 'chora', which they present as a social space in which tourists may interact in creative ways, thus opening to many possibilities. For example, tourist spaces, such as girlfriend getaways, have been described as gendered spaces in which women can embody sisterhood practices, relax and challenge gender power relations (e.g. Kong et al., 2022). Likewise, Fullagar (2008) has insightfully illustrated how some leisure spaces, as sites of playful social encounters, allow women to challenge social norms and, in turn, attain empowerment. In the shared experience of preparing, cooking and eating food in Thailand, creative tourists hinted at multisensory experiences of togetherness or interpersonal existential authenticity (Walter, 2017).

As opposed to the concept of place, which entails fixity and stability (de Certeau, 1984), Wearing and Wearing (1996) maintain that the 'chora' is 'a space whose meaning can be constantly redefined by its inhabitants' (p. 235). These commentators, therefore, advance that understanding the tourist space as 'chora' underscores the importance of social interactions as part of the tourist experience. This resonates with a Deleuzian reading of space that emphasises the relational and fluid character of all processes and forces at play in places. However, the 'chora' seems to emphasise the social and downplays the non-human in the tourist experience. A new materialist understanding of the creative tourist space calls for acknowledging the entanglement of minds, moving bodies, physical and social environments and non-human agents. In this chapter, we will therefore argue that the creative tourist environment should be understood as a transient, social, relational space, which affords creative tourists opportunities to learn about themselves, others and the world around them, as well as to negotiate their embodied identities. In the following two sections, firstly, we will present creative tourist spaces as both regulated and heterogenous. Here, we will argue that creative spaces have liminoid and heterotopic qualities that are conducive to positive change in the individuals who dwell in them. Secondly, we will emphasise the link between creative spaces and experiences of authenticity and intimacy.

4.1 Liminoid Tourist Spaces as Heterotopias

Some tourism spaces are endowed with diacritical atmospheric qualities, which offer experiences to those who wish to escape the routines and strains of everyday life. Furthermore, some tourism spaces allow for greater freedom beyond that which is normally acceptable in other spaces. For that reason, often tourism spaces are thought of as zones of excess and indulgence (Cohen & Cohen, 2019). A recurrent description of tourism spaces that evokes their transitional nature and the licentious behaviours that these spaces afford is that of *liminoid*. Derived from the concept of liminality, which Turner (1979) explains as 'a state or process which is betwixt-and-between the normal, day-to-day cultural and social states and processes of getting and spending, preserving law and order, and registering structural status' (p. 465), liminoid corresponds to a spatial and temporal transitional state in secular modern life. Contrary to liminality, which occurs cyclically in the form of rituals marking a socio-cultural shift in life (e.g. wedding or college graduation), liminoid phenomena happen continuously (Turner, 1974). A liminoid space, therefore, is the one that lies between two other spaces, such as the holiday time spent away from home. For their temporality and the particular performances that tourist spaces offer, liminoid tourist experiences are marked by playfulness and a sense of intimacy or *communitas*.

This is not to say that tourism and leisure spaces are merely synonymous with sites of freedom, hedonistic pleasures and play. In fact, tourism spaces often follow commercial imperatives, which through social norms and regulations, compel tourists to follow designated routes and adopt prescribed behaviours (Edensor, 2006). This is evident in many Thai cooking schools, which rely on standardised processes, speed and efficiency to deliver smooth and playful experiences to culinary tourists. Mills (2019) observes that, in cooking classes, the visible, labour-intensive preparatory work of skilled support staff, such as removing dirty pots, soaking and steaming rice and peeling and carving fruits, makes the most earnest creative tourists 'question the depth and scope of the culinary knowledge on offer' (p. 51). Even though some places, like the Thai cooking schools, may be likened to a stage entertaining scripted performances, tourist spaces are brought about by a whole range of affordances that a stage cannot contain (Massey, 2005, cited in Rankin & Collins, 2017). Not all touristic settings, however, impose discipline on those who enter them. In fact, a host of tourist settings facilitate sensuous and idiosyncratic encounters with places, objects, people and self. Gnoth and Matteucci (2014) similarly remark that some environments are more prone to generate stronger emotions than others. Some tourism spaces, therefore, may unsettle, affect and disrupt sensualities to make those dwelling in them question existing modes of being (Edensor, 2006).

The diversity of creative tourist spaces is reflected in Edensor's (2006) distinction between tourist enclaves and heterogenous spaces. While tourist enclaves relate to highly regulated, contrived tourist environments, in which host-guest relations are heavily orchestrated and transactional, heterogenous spaces, for being seemingly disordered, afford a vast range of sensual and serendipitous experiences. Many spaces, in fact, are endowed with the characteristics of both tourist enclaves and heterogenous sites. Examples of tourist heterogeneous sites abound. For instance, Csikszentmihalyi (2013) acknowledges the sensuous tourist experience of otherness when strolling the alleys of an Arab city with its unique sights, sounds and smells. Edensor and Falconer (2011) describe the peregrinations of backpackers through the sensually rich and drastically unfamiliar, rugged environments of Thai and Indian villages. By way of further illustration, in Matteucci's (2017) work, the streets of Seville in Andalusia are the host of a vast array of sensations from the smell of horse manure, the sound of flamenco music, the sights of children and strollers in public places and to the kinaesthetic sensations of dancing rhythmic sevillanas in cramped spaces at local bars. Because creative tourists tend to seek out experiences that are off the tourism map, creative tourist spaces are not only confined to the classroom. In creative experiences of batá drumming (Windress, 2016), or of sabar dancing (Bizas, 2014), foreign tourists are sometimes invited to stay at their teacher's home. In a similar vein, Bell (2015) provides an insightful account of the domestic spaces in which cooking classes unfold. Here, Bell depicts the Balinese home-cooking environment:

> The classes in private houses took place amidst family activity. For instance, each of these classes coincided with children arriving home from school for lunch and seeking something to eat in the kitchen. They helped themselves from the saucepans and bowls of food we had cooked. Elderly relatives wandered in and out. The space itself was homely, with the everyday items of any ordinary Balinese family. The hostess addressing family members in Bahasa Bali was a reminder of our own outsider or guest status, but also reinforced that it was really a local family in their own dwelling. In that context, language becomes a mechanism to establish and affirm territoriality and authority over the domestic space.

The Balinese home-cooking classes are presented as spaces where multiple social domains interweave: the private, the commercial and hospitality towards guests. Drawing from a personal experience, I (Matteucci) recall taking percussion lessons at my teacher's home in Seville, which allowed me to penetrate the socio-cultural fabrics of a local artist's everyday life. To reach my teacher's home far away from the touristy centre of Seville, I remember being car-driven by my teacher across heterogeneous suburban areas, unknown to me, to eventually find myself in my teacher's kitchen sitting on a cajón (drum box). Not only the car ride gave rise to open conversations that were beyond the typical tourist-host interaction, but also, like Windress in Cuba, I felt I had become a cultural insider, having the privilege to access the domestic sphere of my host, a private sphere that is usually reserved to friends and relatives. Of course, I was well aware that I was granted access to my teacher's home environment, only because of the necessity to teach percussion in a non-rented space. In the eyes of my teacher, I must have remained a tourist who had travelled to Spain to learn percussion and who would return home. Whether regulated and contrived or heterogeneous and kaleidoscopic, creative tourist environments, like many other tourist sites, offer imaginative and enacted alternatives to normative everyday spaces. Such sites have been construed as heterotopias by philosopher and social theorist Michel Foucault (1986).

Foucault distinguishes utopias that he characterises as 'fundamentally unreal spaces' (p. 24) from heterotopias, which he conceives as real spaces in which utopian concepts and ideals of social life can be enacted. For Foucault, heterotopias are counter-sites or alternative sites to mainstream socio-cultural spaces. Examples of heterotopia provided by Foucault are cemeteries, bars, brothels, retirement homes, prisons, fairs, ships and tourist resorts, amongst others. Foucault has articulated six principles of heterotopias. Firstly, although they can take different shapes and forms, heterotopias are found in all cultures; yet, a common feature of the variegated forms of heterotopias is that such sites invite behaviours that, to various degrees, transgress socio-cultural norms. Secondly, the function of a heterotopia may change overtime. In the context of the Montenegrin island of Ada Bojana, Matteucci (2022) illustrates this second principle by tracing the multiple ways people have used wooden river cabins, from accommodating fishermen's activities to indulging in relaxation, nature contemplation and nudism, to hosting tourists' private parties. Thirdly, in heterotopias, several disparate real sites can be juxtaposed in a single space. Foucault (1986) provides the example of exotic gardens that often accommodate an eclectic set of plants and architectural elements from different continents, with each of those carrying different symbolic meanings. The creative tourism context of home-cooking classes, as presented by Mills (2019), similarly illustrates the compound space of both a teacher's suburban home with framed photographs of her children and a commercial setting with scenes of past cooking classes with celebrity chefs and English-language news clippings about the school on display. Fourthly, heterotopias are marked by temporal discontinuities with their full potential being when 'men arrive at a sort of absolute break with their traditional time' (p. 26). Either heterotopias accumulate multiple temporalities (e.g. artefacts from different periods exposed in a museum) or they are transient (e.g. the transitory time of a workshop). Fifthly, their openness and closure characterise heterotopias in that while one may freely enter and exit them, once inside, one is detached from other spaces. Sixthly, heterotopias are spaces of illusion and compensation. In other words, heterotopias either offer the illusion of a perfect social order or they serve as a site of escape and release from the everyday grind. This inversion of the everyday is reflected in Pamela's experience of tango dance instruction and practice in Buenos Aires. Pamela, an American creative tourist who booked a three-day tango experience with a local artist, expresses her transgressive experience as follows: 'For that week, we were completely different people than our normal selves, taking dance lessons and dancing in the milongas until 2 in the morning!'. In short, as Sacco et al. (2019) put it, Foucault's heterotopias 'question existing relations and create a moment of displacement, disconnection from an existing social, cultural and aesthetic order' (p. 201).

This brief introduction to heterotopias will help us articulate a conceptualisation of the creative tourist space as fluid, transient and agentic. Concordant with Topinka's (2010) work on heterotopias, we will argue that creative tourist spaces are 'spatial organs of knowledge production' (p. 66). We now turn our attention to the ways creative tourist spaces invite individuals to sensually engage in playful activities, meet and connect with peers and locals, and sometimes cross their boundaries; hence, below, we articulate the creative tourist space as *local intensities* (Saldanha, 2008) that affect those who dwell in them.

4.2 Play

To illustrate the creative tourist space as a site of resistance (Foucault, 1986), hence a site of self-empowerment, we draw from a range of qualitative studies, which have explored creative tourist experiences in various contexts such as salsa dance classes in Cuba (Menet, 2020), flamenco dance and music in Seville

(Matteucci, 2012, 2014), batá drumming in Cuba (Windress, 2016), cooking classes in Thailand (Mills, 2019; Walter, 2017) and in Bali (Bell, 2015), and sabar dance classes in Senegal (Bizas, 2014). A common thread to all of these studies is that the creative tourist experience offers a social space in which individuals can grow, play, derive meaning and negotiate and reaffirm their embodied identities.

As a central feature of liminoid experiences, play underlies much of creative tourist practices. In Mills' (2019) study, many Thai cooking schools strive to provide a jolly atmosphere to enliven social exchange between cooks and creative participants and among participants themselves. A sense of playfulness is achieved through sexy jokes and entertaining banter. While not all schools deploy the same strategies, Mills notes that 'the playfulness of tourist cooking classes fosters a permissive sensibility, promoting an enjoyable encounter with authentic culinary knowledge' (p. 53). Walter (2017) similarly emphasises the cheerfully festive atmosphere of cooking lessons with tourists having fun 'pounding peppers in a stone pestle, getting their hands wet squeezing coconut milk out of pulp, and stir-frying vegetables in a flash of fire in the open air' (p. 373). This collective fun channelled through embodied performances (as Thai cooking students) is conducive to experiences of togetherness, a kind of 'backstage communitas' with instructors and fellow students. The many stories shared by creative tourists on the VAWAA platform (https://vawaa.com/stories) provide further evidence of the playful character of the creative tourist experience. For instance, Luisa (UK) mentions 'loads of giggles' and Kim Marie (Vietnam) speaks of 'laughter' while harvesting indigo and dyeing textiles in Vietnam. Furthermore, in the same Vietnamese context, Andrew (USA) alludes to play when he says that despite 'having a decent amount of weaving experience', he had 'quite a hilarious time fitting into the back strap floor loom'.

Play can manifest itself in other ways. For instance, in Matteucci's (2012) study, Robert, a French Canadian, who had come to Seville to learn the flamenco guitar, recalls his serendipitous encounter with Monica, a Spanish woman he had met on his way back from his guitar lesson:

> At some point, I was walking when I met this Spanish woman. That was an intense moment too. That was fun … She was sitting there and we started to talk. She was called Monica … I don't think she would have talked to me if I had been with my partner [laugh] and me either actually [laugh] … Yeah, that was fully sexual, sensual and intense. Monica was beautiful and she was just as passionate as any Canadian girl but with a Spanish accent. (p. 127)

The words articulated by Robert connote a reverie of seduction, where bodies and fantasies are entangled. Here, playfulness carries a flirty tone with Monica's physique and her Spanishness in the backdrop. With a hint of embarrassment, however justified by the liminoid environment in which he finds himself, Robert admits having transgressed his own normative behaviour. Imagination may take the form of romance, which appears to be a significant element in the tourist-host encounter. Playful and seductive encounters are also revealed in West African dance classes (Bizas, 2014) and in salsa dancing workshops. Menet (2020) examines the experiences of Western salsa learners in Cuba. She notes that some salsa learners engage in sensual, playful performances as a means to compensate for something that may be missing in their everyday lives. Gendered performances of femininity and masculinity allow tourists to escape the norms of their Western cultures through playful relations on the dance floor. Thus, the liminoid, hetero-topic environment of the salsa workshop offers a social critique of society. At the same time, Menet observes how dancers conform to salsa stereotypes whereby male dancers are expected to play a leading role whereas female dancers take on a following role. When dancers happen to switch roles, switching is legitimised as a playful, didactic tool or as a way to put oneself in the shoes of the dancing partner in order to hone some skills either as leader or follower. Menet concludes that '[b]y constantly marking women leaders and men followers as exceptions, the binary gender structure of salsa dance is actually validated' (p. 109). As Shields (1992) notes, creative spaces are liminoid in character in that they offer neither genuine freedom nor absolute control. The salsa workshop is, thus, revealed as a liminoid space in which gendered identities are enacted playfully, yet without questioning the heteronormative structure of the dance.

4.3 Authenticity

The creative tourist space, such as the salsa and flamenco classes, is often considered as a 'must experience' in tourists' serious leisure trajectories. In the context of salsa dance classes, Menet (2020) asserts that for most tourists, taking classes and dancing with Cubans is seen as a rare opportunity to experience the 'real Cuba'. Likewise, for the flamenco tourists, Seville is described as 'the holy place of flamenco where one must come to in order to experience authentic flamenco' (Matteucci, 2013, p. 113). Irene, one creative tourist from Canada refers to Seville in the following terms:

> Well, on a first thought that came to my mind, I wouldn't be able to do it anywhere else. This energy doesn't exist for me anywhere else … and the presence of flamenco in so many different forms. (Matteucci & Filep, 2017, p. 44)

As the quote indicates, according to flamenco aficionados like Irene, in Seville, there is something in the air that is very flamenco, or in other words, flamenco is an intrinsic quality of Seville, something that is palpable in many spheres of Sevillian social life. Like for the salsa learners for whom taking lessons with Cuban instructors in Cuba brings about the promise of authentic experiences, the flamenco tourists authenticate their experiences through the birth place of their instructors who are either born in Seville or somewhere else within Andalusia. In the case of Western students who travel to Senegal to learn West African dances, authenticity is similarly articulated as a standard for choosing indigenous teachers and dances (Bizas, 2014). One of Bizas' research participants, a woman from New York, expresses her search for 'context' when she says: 'I'm really interested in learning the depth of the dances, what they mean and how they're expressed in context… and not just physically how to do them' (p. 70).

It is apparent that, for creative tourists, learning from local artists is paramount to having a quality and authentic experience. This geographical authenticity is reflected in Anna's words when she says that she came to Seville to immerse herself in the flamenco culture, 'because here during the lessons you meet the true flamencos, who will sing during the lessons and who will share this [...] vivid flamenco thing with you'. As the words articulated by Anna intimate, authenticity needs to be understood as a fluid concept that is largely dependent on the tourist's imaginary and desires towards places, people and cultural manifestations. 'We also experienced Buenos Aires in a way we never otherwise would have had access to' commented Kjell, an American creative tourist on the VAWAA platform. This quote from Kjell's story reveals the creative tourist experience as an authentic time spent from a local perspective. The link between authenticity and the 'local' is also evidenced in the way the VAWAA platform introduces Viviana, a local tango artist: 'Tango is in Viviana's genes. Born and raised in Buenos Aires, mecca of tango, Viviana has been a tango instructor and performer since 1993'. As can be seen in creative tourists' accounts of salsa, flamenco, batá drumming, West African dance, traditional food cooking classes and the many stories shared via the VAWAA platform, the authenticity sought after by many tourists often resides in the history and geographic location of cultural phenomena (Gibson & Connell, 2005).

To better understand creative tourists' imaginaries, practices and experiences, we deem necessary to briefly discuss the ways authenticity has been conceptualised within tourism studies. For that purpose, Wang's (1999) seminal work on authenticity is useful. Wang presents three interpretations of the notion of authenticity, out of which two are based on tourists' perceptions towards objects or artefacts. Wang refers to these two object-based notions of authenticity as *objective authenticity* and *constructive authenticity*. Objective authenticity has to do with the unique properties or the originality of displayed objects (e.g. objects exhibited in museums). Constructive authenticity draws from a less naive position, hence not referring to the originality of objects, but regards an artefact authentic based on its construction and representation by curators, marketers, service providers or artists. Wang's third understanding of the notion of authenticity is not related to objects, services or places as such; instead, it is concerned with tourists' subjective feelings about their lived experiences. This third perspective is referred to as *existential authenticity* because tourists may feel authentic as they are physically and emotionally aroused by certain activities. All three forms of authenticity may be interwoven in the creative tourist experience; yet, existential authenticity often prevails as illustrated in many studies of cultural tourists' experiences. For instance, Ravenscroft and Matteucci (2003) found that for cultural tourists attending the San Fermín fiestas in Pamplona, Navarre, authenticity did not reside in the representation of the event; instead, authenticity was revealed as a function of the intensity of the participants' emotional experience. Other researchers have come to similar conclusions. In his study on La Mercè, a traditional event in Barcelona, Catalonia, Richards (2007) reported that authenticity relates to the tourists' enjoyment of the festival and to the experience of cultural difference.

Prior to Wang's description of existential authenticity, Daniel (1996) had already suggested the term *experiential authenticity* to characterise the deeply emotional experiences that tourists undergo by fully and creatively engaging in dance acts with local performers in Haiti and Cuba. Daniel observes that:

> The experience of performing, especially the experience of danc-ing, is ultimately a route towards genuineness: That space and time where the energy within a dance performance deepens from a routine presentation to a more intense and intensively experienced performance by both the performer and the viewer. (p. 794)

Akin to Wang's existential authenticity and to Daniel's experiential authentic-ity, the term *imaginative unification*, coined by American philosopher and psy-chologist John Dewey (1934), similarly captures this ineffable feeling of unity. For Dewey, imaginative unification corresponds to the state when 'we are car-ried out beyond ourselves to find ourselves' (Bond & Stinson, 2000, p. 73). The vocabulary used by Gilles Deleuze to describe this process would be *deterrito-rialisation* and *reterritorialisation*. This process is visible in the creative tourist experience of flamenco, as Matteucci and Filep (2017) note, 'flamenco activities take tourists away from their ordinary life through states of intense emotional and sensory arousals to then throw them back into a more meaningful life' (p. 48). An existentially authentic experience is a subjective, embodied and contextual process that one undergoes while engaging in intrinsically motivated, identity-related activities. Participating in non-habitual tourist performances creates instances for reflection and is likely to foster explicit awareness. In other words, embodied feelings of authenticity are difficult to verbalise, yet such experiences can be reflected upon and, in turn, inform us about what is involved in crea-tive tourists' performances. From the discipline of psychology, Waterman (2005) refers to a comparable experiential process as *personal expressiveness*. Waterman suggests that while partaking in intrinsically motivated activities like tourists' dance performances, individuals 'experience (a) an unusual intense involvement, (b) a special fit or meshing with the activities, (c) a feeling of intensely being alive, (d) a feeling of completeness or fulfilment, (e) an impression that this is what the person was meant to do, and (f) a feeling that this is what the person really is' (p. 169). While this description reminds us of *flow* (Csikszentmihalyi, 1990) and of *performative authenticity* (Knudsen & Waade, 2010), personal expressive-ness is less hedonistic and more eudaimonic in character because, by engaging in meaningful activities, creative tourists feel authentic in that they are (re)connect-ing with their true nature. Below, the excerpt from Maya about her experience of dancing during a flamenco lesson illustrates the intense and meaningful feeling of existential authenticity:

> It is a particular moment in time where the notion of time, space and everything is absent. You're suspended like that in the air, [a moment] where you can concentrate all your energy, all what the music inspires you, all that passion that you feel inside and also

all these things that you feel because of what you went through, you can invest all that within a few seconds. It's like something suspended out of time. There is nothing more enriching than this, and priceless. (Matteucci, 2018, p. 15)

The fourth principle of heterotopia, according to Foucault (1986), is to mark a break with traditional time, a facet that is clearly revealed in Maya's account when she says she feels 'suspended out of time'. The creative tourism literature provides other insightful accounts of tourists' experiences of authenticity. In peripheral and less populated areas of Chiang Mai, Mills (2019) describes how the picturesque and tranquil rurality of some Thai farmers' market spaces and the rusticity of some cooking schools with their own vegetable gardens imbue the creative tourist experience with a sense of authenticity. Visits to farmers' markets are punctuated with vivid, multisensory experiences that assure visitors that they are experiencing the 'real' thing (Mills, 2019). Narrow market aisles are flanked by variegated food stalls, displaying piles of fresh, colourful and irregular-shaped produce, alternating sweet aromatic scents of exotic fruits with fishy, pungent smells. Authenticity is associated with unstaged, unsanitised and even sometimes offensive impressions pertaining to heterogeneous spaces like Thai farmers' markets. By way of further illustration, in rural Bali, Indonesia, creative tourists find whiffs of authenticity in the domestic realm of home-cooking classes. As Bell (2015) notes, the rice paddy outside the home-cooking school provides tourists with 'a taste of "real Bali"' (p. 92). Entering the backstage of a Balinese family's domestic environment gives creative tourists the opportunity to 'share the kitchen bench, the sink and the simple wok over the gas burner' (p. 94). A sense of authenticity is also magnified if tourists sensually encounter non-Western amenities and the occasional lizards moving swiftly up the walls (Bell, 2015).

In home-cooking classes, authenticity is further facilitated by the physical proximity of hosts and guests, the sharing of utensils for peeling, grating, cutting and the sharing of life stories. In the context of West African dance classes, an authentic experience is an experience of sensual proximity, which is facilitated by a total immersion into an African village where the workshops take place. Bizas (2014) observes that '[e]xperiencing Senegalese life means living the way local people do and engaging in their everyday activities' (p. 75). Mary, one dance tourist in Dakar, reports: 'we stayed with a family and so really got the real deal – the toilets, the mosque, the imams waking you up in the morning' (p. 75). By way of further illustration, authenticity, in terms of full immersion in the private sphere of the hosts, is insightfully narrated by Bizas in the following description of her sabar teacher's house in Dakar, Senegal:

Ashtou's house was in Pikine, a poor district on the outskirts of Dakar. Her room was on the top floor of a two-storey building. There were four rooms on each floor, all with a large bed, a few suitcases on top of a wardrobe and a big coloured television. The complex housed Ashtou's extended family, and slept around four people per bed. They shared the upstairs toilet and the ground floor cooking area with a fridge in the enclosed courtyard. The walls of the courtyard were worn out and inscribed with telephone numbers detached from any names they might belong to. Broken mirror pieces were screwed on the wall, where women would gather to apply their make-up. Colourful clothes would be hung to dry in the courtyard, which was full of children, friends and neighbours, as women chatted and gossiped over cooking and ironing. Outside the complex were the sandy streets that are so typical of Dakar. Ashtou's grandmother kept a stand there, from where she sold Senegalese snacks and seasonal fruit, a characteristic initiative by Senegalese women to maintain their own income. She was not required to watch the stand constantly, as any neighbours or family members who were hanging around would always help potential customers. (p. 91)

This lengthy quotation evokes the power of heterogeneous spaces in facilitating an authentic, intimate understanding of the hosts' culture and context. For those creative tourists partaking in dance classes in Western Africa, Bizas (2014) notes, the Western African 'context of the dance form has direct implications on the self' in that the 'context can be used as currency, to legitimise self to oneself and to others in the practice of the dance form' (p. 71). This reflects the view that one can only truly understand the dance form in the context from which it originates. While creative tourism cannot be entirely free from economic imperatives, creative tourist settings are spaces of conviviality where people meet, drink, eat and socialise, thus forging new modes of living and being together. Hence, the creative tourist experience offers a more sincere, hospitable space beyond that of the ubiquitous staged hospitality of the tourism industry. So far, we have seen that authenticity has been expressed in terms of geography, historicity, off the beaten track, unsanitised, multisensory experiences and in terms of the intensity of emotions felt through performances. Another central dimension of authenticity relates to the intimate socialities that creative tourist spaces afford.

4.4 Intimacy

For their social, spatial and atmospheric qualities, some holiday and leisure spaces are conducive to interpersonal experiences of closeness and connection. Intimacy, also expressed as *communitas* by Turner (1974), is an intrinsic feature of liminoid environments. Although traditionally associated with the bonds that tie family members, romantic couples and friends, intimacy has been recently interpreted as a broader and more fluid concept that refers to specific modes of interaction that bring people together (Törnqvist, 2018). Like creativity, intimacy is a multidimensional concept (Jamieson, 1999), which relates to different realms of experience. Trauer and Ryan (2005) explain that intimacy can be experienced through physical contact, verbal communication, intellectual exchange and a spiritual connection with other people. These commentators argue that, through leisure travel, what the majority of people may be looking for is, in fact, a privileged space that offers opportunities for sharing and bonding with meaningful others. A number of other scholars have subscribed to this view and have provided empirical evidence that tourism spaces are fertile ground for nurturing relationships and for promoting experiences of intimacy (e.g. Heimtun, 2007; Matteucci, Volić, & Filep, 2022).

In the creative tourist experience, intimacy can take different shapes and forms. The intimate socialities of some creative spaces such as home-cooking schools, dance floors, workshops, community centres and the nooks and crannies of cities afford liminoid performances and experiences of attachment. In Bell's (2015) study, the private, sometimes modest, space of the home-cooking schools in Bali offers Western tourists a rupture of their everyday life; the sensuality of the backstage experience of the Balinese family kitchen lays ground for a fleeting moment of felt intimacy shared with strangers. The creative space of the home-cooking school is an open window to the private sphere of Balinese dwellers; it enables tourists to make sense of local activities through acts of sharing kitchenware, food and personal life stories. Bell observes that 'the lessons that took place felt less like a professional exchange and more like friends cooking together, with the local person in charge' (p. 95). She adds that '[t]he relationship being enacted was that of host and guest rather than customer and proprietor' (p. 95). In the private environment of the home-cooking schools, intimacy therefore alludes to a space of hospitality and conviviality.

A sense of conviviality and the comfort of the domestic sphere of artists' studios are similarly found in many accounts of creative tourists' experiences on the VAWAA platform. For instance, Felissa (USA) refers to her time with Chikako, a Japanese calligraphy artist, in the following terms:

> We really loved getting to know Chikako and spending time with her. It was really special to be in Chikako's studio, surrounded by her and her mother's artwork. We loved meeting her mother, who is herself a calligraphy master and lovely, warm teacher. Having lunch with Chikako everyday and trading stories was delightful and a highlight of our time in Kyoto. Chikako also recommended some spots in Kyoto, and prepared delicious teas and snacks for us everyday.

As Felissa's testimony attests, the sharing of life stories and open, sincere communication may also translate into experiences of closeness or intimacy. For instance, at a cooking school in Thailand, through telling stories of her own rugged life trajectory, Mills (2019) reports how a teacher was able to produce an atmosphere of openness and informality and, in turn, to convey a feeling of comfort and a sense of relatedness. In preparation for cooking classes, culinary tourists are sometimes taken to food markets where they can experience spaces of hospitality. As Anderson (2004) argues, the food market space allows 'practical and expressive folk ethnography' (p. 21). Anderson notes that, in the somehow sheltered and semi-bounded spaces of food markets, people are more inclined to look at each other, chat, hence the market affords hospitable relations to unfold. While in many commercial spaces of creative tourism, it would be legitimate to question the sincerity underpinning enactments of hospitality, D. Bell (2007) maintains that forms of hospitality between hosts and guests are not solely and necessarily confined to monetary exchange. Even though host-guest interactions may not ineluctably produce a deep sense of belonging among participants, D. Bell warns of the risk of dismissing the mundane moments of togetherness pertaining to some host-guest encounters, which, he argues, may promote new forms of socialities such as 'new solidarities and new collectivities' (Latham, 2003, p. 1719). The following quotation from Di, a British creative tourist, provides an evocative example of a sincere and deeper form of sociality than that of most tourist-host encounters:

> We also had many heart to heart conversations through the week about art and craft, design and culture, and life per se. It's really a very memorable trip and I hope I'll be back to Vietnam to visit Thao again in the near future!

The social and intimate dimensions of creative tourism can also be highlighted using examples of dance and music. This includes interactions and connections between creative tourists and local communities. For example, Aterianus-Owanga (2019) shows how sabar dance is used as a 'transcultural connector dissolving cultural borders' encouraging greater social interaction and intimacy (p. 15). In the creative tourist experience of batá drumming in Cuba, Windress (2016) notes that learners and teachers can develop a cultural understanding and empathy for the 'other' (p. 133). While Windress also recognises that student-teacher relations may be tainted by economic inequalities, he observes that, in the context of a musical performance, 'a foreigner can come to be accepted as an equal amongst batá drummers, at least for the duration of the performance' (p. 147). This observation warrants attention to the type of friendship deployed between foreigners and locals. Although Windress signals that friendship ties between Western students and their Cuban instructors often transcend mutual musical goals, Jamieson (1999) reminds us that 'few relationships, even friendships, are mainly simply about mutual appreciation, knowing and understanding' (p. 482). Jamieson's remark brings to mind that friendships can be of utility (*cf.* Aristotle) and motivated by self-interest (*cf.* Nietzsche). Jacques Derrida (1994) contributes to this discussion by arguing that, despite their inscrutable differences, individuals may preserve their friendship bond by embracing their enigmatic idiosyncrasies.

In our introduction to this section, we suggested that creative tourist spaces may confer a sense of collective identity on its members. This feeling of connectedness or *communitas* is found in dancers' accounts of 'salsa as an inclusive *community* where people are united through their passion for salsa' (Menet, 2020, p. 2). For example, Menet asks one dancer about what has changed as a result of her creative tourist experience:

> I think about almost everything has changed. [...] Once you enter the scene [...] you get to know so many people. And somehow your life goes there. [...] All of a sudden, all your friends are there and your private life is in that environment. It's not just a hobby, it's different. Also, the worldwide connections, it got so extreme. (p. 55)

In the transnational tango scene, Törnqvist (2018) similarly observes that a strong sense of belonging to 'a new family' is often expressed by aficionados attending tango workshops (p. 359). This feeling of *communitas* is also found in creative tourists' experiences of flamenco. Irene, for instance, speaks of flamenco as a community:

> You know, this flamenco thing, it just reminded me, it's about community too. For example, I have sort of flamenco friends; I call them flamenco friends. I see them only here when I come to Jerez, so it's the third time some of the people that I've seen during the Jerez festival and we connect on Facebook or via email but usually on Facebook. But there is a sense of community which is quite important. So it's not my mainstream life but part of the spirit is very important in my life. Personally … Yeah … to be able to and not only to do it but also to belong to, to belong to a group that has something and it's passionate about it or not [laugh] or have a different take to learn from experiences. And part of it, it is that it is an international group. So it's not only – you know – the generic when it comes to nation, a generic group from Canada or … No, I have friends, flamenco friends, from Moscow, from my own country, from Japan, from Germany, from Poland, from Spain, so … You know, from Italy, girls that like to party [laugh].

When Irene says that the flamenco community is not her 'mainstream life', she alludes to an alternative, fleeting social space that she can enter and leave freely (e.g. dance workshops in Seville or Jerez or Facebook as a virtual space). She refers to a flamenco space, which affords experiences of transitory, playful, collective intimacy that resonates with Foucault's description of heterotopias as counter-sites in which utopian ideals of social life can be enacted. In Törnqvist's (2018) study, the Argentine tango experience is similarly presented as a liminoid space, 'a rupture of everyday life' or a semi-anonymous environment infused with collective fantasies, attachments and an intense sense of being-in-relation (p. 366). Through the 'skin-to-skin texture' of the performance, the tango dance floor 'allows for an intimate presence that is lived through the touch and presence of temporary dance partners, as well as through imagination comporting childhood memories and fragments of lost love' (p. 367). In line with Saldanha's (2008) understanding of heterotopias as permeable spaces of *local intensities*, Törnqvist articulates the intimacy of the creative tango space in terms of a relational quality.

In this chapter, we laid the groundwork for the analysis of the creative tourist experience as eudaimonic and transformational. While not all creative tourist spaces share the same contingent qualities, what the works presented in Chapters 3 and 4 have revealed is that, as heterotopias, heterogenous creative tourist spaces possess the agency to foster positive emotions and positive change in those who dwell in them.

References

Amirou, R. (1994). Le tourisme comme objet transitionnel. *Espaces et Sociétés, 76,* 149–164. doi:10.3917/esp.1994.76.0149

Amirou, R. (1995). *Imaginaire touristique et sociabilités du voyage.* Paris: Presses Universitaires de France.

Anderson, E. (2004). The cosmopolitan canopy. *Annals of the American Academy of Political and Social Science, 595,* 14–31. doi:10.1177/0002716204266833

Aterianus-Owanga, A. (2019). 'KAAY FECC!' (Come Dance!): Economic, cultural and emotional flows in the 'dance tourism' of *sabar* (Senegal-Europe). In M. Kaag, G. Khan-Mohammad, & S. Schmid (Eds.), *Destination Africa – Contemporary Africa as a centre of global encounter* (pp. 148–168). Leiden: Brill.

Bell, D. (2007). The hospitable city: Social relations in commercial spaces. *Progress in Human Geography, 31*(1), 7–22. doi:10.1177/0309132507073526

Bell, C. (2015). Tourists infiltrating authentic domestic space at Balinese home cooking schools. *Tourist Studies, 15*(1), 86–100. doi:10.1177/1468797614550958

Bizas, E. (2014). *Learning Senegalese Sabar: Dancers and embodiment in New York and Dakar.* London: Berghahn Books.

Bond, K. E., & Stinson, S. W. (2000). 'I feel like I'm going to take off!' Young people's experiences of the superordinary in dance. *Dance Research Journal, 32*(2), 52–87. doi:10.2307/1477981

Boorstin, D. J. (1964). *The image: A guide to pseudo-events in America.* New York, NY: Harper & Row.

Caltabiano, P. A. (2009). Embodied identities: Negotiating the self through flamenco dance. *Anthropology Theses, 33.* http://digitalarchive.gsu.edu/anthro_theses/33/

Cohen, S. A., & Cohen, E. (2019). New directions in the sociology of tourism. *Current Issues in Tourism, 22*(2), 153–172. doi:10.1080/13683500.2017.1347151

Crouch, D., Aronsson, L., & Wahlström, L. (2001). Tourist encounters. *Tourist Studies, 1*(3), 253–270. doi:10.1177/146879760100100303

Csikszentmihalyi, M. (1990). *Flow: The psychology of optimal experience.* New York, NY: Harper and Row.

Csikszentmihalyi, M. (2013). Foreword. In S. Filep & P. Pearce (Eds.), *Tourist experience and fulfilment: Insights from positive psychology.* Oxon: Routledge.

Daniel, Y. P. (1996). Tourism dance performances: Authenticity and creativity. *Annals of Tourism Research, 23,* 780–797. doi:10.1016/0160-7383(96)00020-5

De Certeau, M. (1984). *The practice of everyday life* (Trans. S. Rendall). Berkeley, CA: University of California Press.

Derrida, J. (1994). *Politiques de l'amitié, suivi de L'oreille de Heidegger.* Paris: Galilée.

Dewey, J. (1934). *A common faith.* Hanover: Yale University Press.

Edensor, T. (2006). Sensing tourist spaces. In C. Minca & T. Oakes (Eds.), *Travels in paradox: Remapping tourism* (pp. 23–46). London: Rowman and Littlefield.

Edensor, T., & Falconer, E. (2011). Sensual geographies of tourism. In J. Wilson (Ed.), *The Routledge handbook of tourism geographies* (pp. 74–81). London: Routledge.

Foucault, M. (1986). Of other spaces. *Diacritics, 16*(1), 22–27.

Fullagar, S. (2008). Leisure practices as counter-depressants: Emotion-work and emotion-play within women's recovery from depression. *Leisure Sciences, 30,* 35–52. doi:10.1080/01490400701756345

Gibson, C., & Connell J. (2005). *Music and tourism, on the road again.* Clevedon, OH: Channel View Publications.

Gnoth, J., & Matteucci, X. (2014). Response to Pearce and McCabe's critiques. *International Journal of Culture, Tourism and Hospitality Research, 8*(2), 242–251. doi:10.1108/IJCTHR-04-2014-0029

Grosz, E. (1995). Women, *chora*, dwelling. In S. Watson & K. Gibson (Eds.), *Postmodern cities and spaces* (pp. 47–58). Oxford: Blackwell.

Heimtun, B. (2007). Depathologizing the tourist syndrome: Tourism as social capital production. *Tourist Studies, 7*(3), 271–293. doi:10.1177/1468797608092513

Jamieson, L. (1999). Intimacy transformed? A critical look at the 'pure relationship'. *Sociology, 33*(3), 477–494. doi:10.1177/S0038038599000310

Knudsen, B. T., & Waade, A. M. (Eds.). (2010). *Re-investing authenticity: Tourism, place and emotions*. Bristol: Channel View.

Kong, S., Guo, J., & Huang, D. (2022). The girlfriend getaway as an intimacy. *Annals of Tourism Research, 92*, 103337. doi:10.1016/j.annals.2021.103337

Latham, A. (2003). Urbanity, lifestyle and making sense of the new urban cultural economy: Notes from Auckland, New Zealand. *Urban Studies, 40*, 1699–1724. doi:10.1080/0042098032000106564

Massey, D. (2005). *For space*. London: Sage.

Matteucci, X. (2012). The tourist experience of intangible heritage: The case of flamenco consumers. Unpublished doctoral dissertation, Vienna University of Economics and Business (WU), Vienna.

Matteucci, X. (2013). Experiencing flamenco: An examination of a spiritual journey. In S. Filep & P. Pearce (Eds.), *Tourist experience and fulfilment: Insights from positive psychology* (pp. 110–126). London: Routledge.

Matteucci, X. (2014). Forms of body usage in tourists' experiences of flamenco. *Annals of Tourism Research, 46*, 29–43. doi:10.1016/j.annals.2014.02.005

Matteucci, X. (2017). Tourists' accounts of learning and positive emotions through sensory experiences. In S. Filep, J. Laing, & M. Csikszentmihalyi (Eds.), *Positive tourism* (pp. 54–67), London: Routledge.

Matteucci, X. (2018). Flamenco, tourists' experiences, and the meaningful life. In M. Uysal, J. Sirgy, & S. Kruger (Eds.), *Managing quality of life in tourism and hospitality* (pp. 10–23). Wallingford: CABI.

Matteucci, X. (2022). Female friends' holiday experiences in heterotopia. *Journal of Qualitative Research in Tourism, 3*(1), 14–31. doi:10.4337/jqrt.2022.01.02

Matteucci, X., & Filep, S. (2017). Eudaimonic tourist experiences: The case of flamenco. *Leisure Studies, 36*(1), 39–52. doi:10.1080/02614367.2015.1085590

Matteucci, X., Volić, I., & Filep, S. (2022). Dimensions of friendship in shared travel experiences. *Leisure Sciences, 44*(6), 697–714. doi:10.1080/01490400.2019.1656121

Menet, J. (2020). *Entangled mobilities in the transnational salsa circuit: The Esperanto of the body, gender and ethnicity*. London: Routledge.

Mills, M. B. (2019). Authentic dishes, staged identities: Thailand's cooking schools for tourists. *Gastronomica, 19*(2), 43–55. doi:10.1525/gfc.2019.19.2.43

Rankin, J. R., & Collins, F. L. (2017). Enclosing difference and disruption: Assemblage, heterotopia and the cruise ship. *Social & Cultural Geography, 18*(2), 224–244. doi:10.1080/14649365.2016.1171389

Ravenscroft, N., & Matteucci, X. (2003). The festival as carnivalesque: Social governance and control at Pamplona's San Fermin fiestas. *Tourism Culture & Communication, 4*(1), 1–15. doi:10.3727/109830403108750777

Richards, G. (2007). Culture and authenticity in a traditional event: The views of producers, residents, and visitors in Barcelona. *Event Management, 11*, 33–44. doi:10.3727/152599508783943228

Sacco, P. L., Ghirardi, S., Tartari, M., & Trimarchi, M. (2019). Two versions of heterotopia: The role of art practices in participative urban renewal processes. *Cities, 89*, 199–208. doi:10.1016/j.cities.2019.02.013

Saldanha, A. (2008). Heterotopia and structuralism. *Environment and Planning A: Economy and Space, 40*(9), 2080–2096. doi:10.1068/a39336

Shields, R. (1992). Spaces for the subject of consumption. In R. Shields (Ed.), *Lifestyle shopping: The subject of consumption* (pp. 1–21). London: Routledge.

Topinka, R. J. (2010). Foucault, Borges, heterotopia: Producing knowledge in other spaces. *Foucault Studies, 9*, 54–70. doi:10.22439/fs.v0i9.3059

Törnqvist, M. (2018). Rethinking intimacy: Semi-anonymous spaces and transitory attachments in Argentine tango dancing. *Current Sociology, 66*(3), 356–372. doi:10.1177/0011392116681385

Trauer, B., & Ryan, C. (2005). Destination image, romance and place experience – An application of intimacy theory in tourism. *Tourism Management, 26*, 481–491. doi:10.1016/j.tourman.2004.02.014

Turner, V. (1974). Liminal to liminoid, in play, flow and ritual: An essay in comparative symbology. In E. Norbeck (Ed.), *The anthropological study of human play* (pp. 53–92). Houston, OH: Rice University Studies.

Turner, V. (1979). Frame, flow and reflection: Ritual and drama as public liminality. *Japanese Journal of Religious Studies*, 6/4 December issue.

Walter, P. (2017). Culinary tourism as living history: Staging, tourist performance and perceptions of authenticity in a Thai cooking school. *Journal of Heritage Tourism, 12*(4), 365–379. doi:10.1080/1743873X.2016.1207651

Wang, N. (1999). Rethinking authenticity in tourism experience. *Annals of Tourism Research, 26*(2), 349–370. doi:10.1016/S0160-7383(98)00103-0

Waterman, A. S. (2005). When effort is enjoyed: Two studies of intrinsic motivation for personally salient activities. *Motivation and Emotion, 29*, 165–188. doi:10.1007/s11031-005-9440-4

Wearing, B., & Wearing, S. (1996). Refocussing the tourist experience: The flâneur and the choraster. *Leisure Studies, 15*, 229–243. doi:10.1080/026143696375530

Wearing, S., Stevenson, D., & Young, T. (2010). *Tourist cultures: Identity, place and the traveller*. London: Sage.

Windress, K. (2016). Musical pilgrimages to Cuba: Negotiating tourism and musical learning in Cuban Batá Drumming. *MUSICultures, 43*(1), 132–152. Retrieved from https://journals.lib.unb.ca/index.php/MC/article/view/25263

Chapter 5

Journeys of Self-development

'I hate tourist traps. I would rather be around locals and enjoy a destination as seen by people who actually LIVE there'. This quote from Michael, an American creative tourist who stayed with and took tango lessons from a local artist in Buenos Aires, reflects the anti-touristic rhetoric that is often found in creative tourists' travel accounts. Those who participate in creative tourism seem to oppose themselves to mainstream cultural tourists who belong to a 'crowd of sheep just going everywhere', as stated by a working artist in Whiting and Hannam's (2014) study (p. 69). This anti-touristic sentiment mirrors a much-debated distinction in the tourism literature, which is the one between the tourist and the traveller. One early description of the Western tourist is provided by Boorstin (1964) who articulates tourists as 'superficial nitwits' (Cohen, 1979, p. 19). In a similar fashion, Onfray (2007) assimilates the tourist to someone who is satisfied with superficial experiences, whereas the traveller is said to be eager to grasp the subtleties of the world that she/he visits from the inside. This distinction is not unimportant as the term 'tourist' implies a trivial hedonistic pursuit while the 'traveller' connotes a certain interest in self-development.

Urbain (2002) dedicates much of his book *L'idiot du Voyage: Histoires de Touristes* discussing this evasive distinction. Urbain contends that, for gazing perplexedly and complacently at sites and cultures that he/she barely understands, the tourist has received bad press, especially within cultural circles. Yet, he argues, the tourist has significantly contributed to expand the notion of culture, both as an exporter and an importer of cultural influences. The tourist stimulates cultural hybridisation and crossbreeding. For instance, the remarkable success of world music is arguably largely indebted to tourists. At the same time, tourists are often blamed for commodifying and destroying the cultures they have come to visit. On the other hand, in the Western imaginary, Urbain notes, the traveller has an elevated status; the one of an anthropologist who blends in with the locals and embarks on a commendable journey of discovery and understanding. While it is important to acknowledge that not all visitors have the same needs and aspirations, the distinction between tourist and traveller seems rather simplistic as tourists can enact a traveller's role and travellers may become tourists during the same trip. The same can be said about the creative tourists whose level of interest and motivation may vary within the same trip and from one trip to another.

The Creative Tourist: A Eudaimonic Perspective, 69–85
Copyright © 2024 by Xavier Matteucci and Melanie Kay Smith
Published under exclusive licence by Emerald Publishing Limited
doi:10.1108/978-1-83753-404-320241005

Whether framed as a search for pleasure, for identity construction, cultural capital or as an escape from the day-to-day existence, what most people may be looking for through travel and tourism is nothing less than a pursuit of happiness (Aramberri, 2001; Urbain, 2007). Happiness in the context of tourism is often associated with short-lived and hedonistic experiences. It is also worth considering the relative value of pleasure, as it has been argued that some pleasures are more valuable than others, for example, moral, intellectual and aesthetic pleasures are often thought to have 'higher value' than bodily pleasures (Heathwood, 2014). However, in the context of creative tourism and especially in dance, the two might be inextricably interconnected. Scholars are increasingly suggesting that tourism can be connected to more eudaimonic concepts such as 'existential authenticity' (Kirillova & Lehto, 2015) and personal transformation (Fu, Tanyatanaboon, & Lehto, 2015). Eudaimonic approaches are thought to be connected to self-development, personal growth and self-fulfilment, as well as optimal performance of meaningful behaviour and full engagement (Cloninger, 2004). Authentic happiness models in the context of tourism would promote forms of tourism that revolve around a combination of pleasure, altruism and meaningful experience (Filep, 2012; Smith & Diekmann, 2017). Creative tourism is considered to be one of these forms of tourism with aspirations towards personal flourishing as well as universal harmony, in accordance with principles of Aristotelian eudaimonia (Sørensen, 2010). It fits well into Ryan and Deci's (2000) Self Determination Theory (SDT) framework that differs from other psychological perspectives in that it emphasises an 'actualising tendency', which means a fundamental motivation towards growth. It posits three psychological needs that determine well-being: Autonomy, competence and relatedness. Such needs can be connected to self-development, mastering a skill, as well as interacting with and helping others (Smith & Diekmann, 2017). Duxbury and Bakas (2021) perceive creative tourism 'as a step towards "humanizing" travel as it includes an ethics of care for the locale in which activities are implemented as well as for the well-being and creative potential of the traveler' (p. 111). While we believe that the well-being of the host community should be at the centre of tourism policy, here because our focus lies on the creative tourist experience, in line with Duxbury and Bakas (2021), we are going to argue that creative tourism offers fertile ground for fostering the eudaimonic well-being of the tourist. Firstly, we will emphasise the link between creative tourism and the construction of personal identities; secondly, we will present the creative tourist experience as an important source of inspiration and as transformational.

5.1 Identity and the Creative Self

In contemporary (post)industrial societies, people may find many outlets for the construction of individual identity. In a global network society, characterised by a vast and fluid array of social interactions and movements, personal identities are unstable, multiple and ever-shifting (Bauman, 2000). Within this context, tourism, and creative tourism in particular, is a rich terrain for individuals to nurture their own identity project. Wearing et al. (2010) have argued that tourism can be understood as 'a process of expanded social interaction whereby self-identity has the potential for enlargement and growth through the engagement of the tourist with other environments, peoples, societies and cultures' (p. 36). In other words, tourism is presented as a socio-cultural space in which individuals can learn new roles, play with and enact role identities as well as cultivate self-awareness. For example, in the previous chapter, we have seen that culinary tourists enjoy performing the role of Thai cooks through their creative participation in cooking activities in Thailand. In Portugal, some tourists enact the role of harvesters and wine makers, and others become ceremonial batá drummers in Cuba. From Onfray's (2007) point of view, the selection of a holiday destination and of the activities to participate in are a reflection of the tourist's multiple identities. It is debateable as to whether there is a 'true' or 'authentic' self to be found as proposed in previous transformational literature (Brown, 2013; Reisinger, 2013; Smith, 2013). Some authors have disagreed about tourists 'finding themselves', arguing that the tourist self is not a fixed entity and is simply created using symbolic products and experiences abroad (Gazley & Watling, 2015). Within a creative tourism context, various selves are explored as identified by Sirgy and Su (2000) including tourists' actual self-image (how people see themselves); ideal self (how they would like to see themselves); social self (how they think others see them); and ideal social self (how they would like others to see them).

In Chapter 3, we have suggested that attending to embodied practices sheds some light on the ways creative tourists negotiate their identities whereby differentiating themselves through the production and reproduction of cultural capital. By attending to the ways in which creative tourists use their bodies, we have shown that through consumptive practices and performances of flamenco dance and music in Seville, creative tourists seek to attain a particular body-image, to fulfil their need for self-expression, to achieve social status and at the same time to resist social norms. Our account of embodied experiences has also revealed that tourists' performances are shaped by a complex mix of personal and socio-cultural factors, such as the myths and fantasies that emanate from the tourist's society. It is, therefore, not uncommon, as noted by Theodossopoulos (2012), that Western tourists experience foreign cultures through their own static, preconceived images of places; places that are thought to be untouched by modernity. Rosaldo (1989) describes this Western sentiment as 'imperialist nostalgia', which, Theodossopoulos (2012) explains, is when 'the children of modernity mourn what was lost by the dominating impact of their own societies' (p. 134). Below, we illustrate the construction of four identities as revealed in different creative tourists' accounts: gendered identity, marginal identity, cultural identity and cosmopolitan identity.

5.1.1 Gendered and Marginal Identities

Creative tourism, as a form of serious leisure, offers a playground for those who wish to achieve a number of personal benefits such as enhancement of self-image, social interaction and belongingness (Stebbins, 1982). Creative tourism spaces tend to be predominantly female, especially in contexts that are offering arts-based experiences like dancing. Creative retreats, for example, tend to attract more than 80% female solo travellers who are middle class, professional and educated (Kelly & Smith, 2016). Thus, the discussion of gendered identities becomes especially pertinent. The tourists' engagement in creative activities in order to enhance their self-image has been documented in experiences of flamenco dance. Some female flamenco tourists, Matteucci (2014) observes, 'strive to relate to an eroticized flamenco body' (p. 34). Tourists' descriptions of the flamenco body converge towards the stereotypical image of the sensual female flamenco dancer, which is ubiquitously presented in the media.

> [In flamenco] I think that the body language is very feminine but still very assertive. For example, I did oriental dance which is also very feminine but there is this teasing and seductive aspect about it which does not suit me. And this is what I like about flamenco, that the woman by staying extremely feminine is assertive. She's not an object. (p. 38)

Above, the words articulated by Céline about being 'feminine' connote ideas of sensuality and desirability which are commonly ascribed to female flamenco dancers. Heffner Hayes (2009) remarks that the social imaginary of the sensual, feminine dancer is strongly embedded in the way flamenco history has been (re)written which depicts the female dancer as a passionate object who, through her lascivious curves, is overly feminine and sexual. This exotic, carnal woman as an object of desire and pleasure is arguably heavily imbued with a masculinised frame of reference. What is interesting though is that whether it is flamenco in Seville, salsa in Cuba, or even salsa in Belfast or Hamburg, Skinner (2007) argues, creative tourism or leisure pursuits more generally reveal 'the force of the imagination, an imagination no longer an antidote to social experience, now a possibility for social action' (p. 489). The creative dance tourist experience, therefore, serves as a catalyst through which tourists can pursue the gendered identities of their imagination. Similar to the female flamenco tourists, the Western females taking salsa dance classes in Cuba embrace the possibility that salsa opens up for them to feel like a woman in their bodies (Menet, 2020). One of these women, Manuela, holds that her upbringing, underpinned by the growing social concern for gender equality, has largely hindered her ability to learn how to follow the lead of men in salsa. Like some Western female flamenco enthusiasts in Seville, outside the salsa classes, Manuela felt 'independent' and 'not feminine'. This connects to the notion of the 'actual self-image' versus the 'ideal' one (Sirgy & Su, 2000). Menet (2020) asserts that salsa dancing can be experienced as a 'compensatory space' for Western women like Manuela (p. 105). Menet goes on to say that some of her female research participants

> actually liked dancing salsa not in spite of but precisely because of its gender arrangements. For them, salsa opens up a space where they can dress up and behave in ways they would not in other social situations, and they clearly mark the context of salsa as specific and different from other social situations in their life. (p. 105)

As discussed in Chapter 4, some creative tourism spaces offer the possibilities for individuals to resist and negotiate social norms. We have argued that the creative tourist experience, therefore, can be viewed as a heterotopia (Foucault, 1986). We have seen some examples of how women use creative dance tourism as a way to embody their feminine self, whereby confronting the Western concern for gender equality, yet paradoxically conforming to gender roles. This idea can be related to the desire to create a 'social self' or an 'ideal social self' in a different cultural context from home (Sirgy & Su, 2000). Creative tourism, however, can similarly be used by men to reinforce their self-concept of masculinity. In the context of creative flamenco tourism, it is noteworthy that the vast majority of male creative tourists enact their masculinity through their choice for the flamenco guitar. Contrary to female tourists, few males opt for the dance (*baile*), and while some choose singing (*cante*), most male tourists travel to Spain to learn the flamenco guitar (*toque*). This echoes Labajo's (2003) observation that women, whether Spanish or foreign, are largely absent from the flamenco guitar scene. Beyond the flamenco guitar, Matteucci (2014) notes that male flamenco tourists embody their masculinity through the consumption of alcohol and the adoption of a particular flamenco look. For instance, by adopting a long wavy hairstyle, some flamenco aficionados conform to the stereotypical image of the contemporary gypsy flamenco artist. Because identities are dynamic, as Gibson and Connell (2005) remind us, they are maintained, contested and 'continually reproduced through a repetitive enactment of expectations and appearances' (p. 151). Not only are flamenco gypsies (gitanos) characterised by their extreme masculinity for their hoarse voices and their excessive consumption of alcohol, tobacco and drugs (Labajo, 2003), but flamenco itself is also a form of expression associated with the *gitanos*, a marginalised social group. By evoking their empathy and relatedness to the troubled history of the gitanos, an oppressed minority group in Spain, the flamenco tourists expressed a sense of marginality through their adherence to the flamenco culture. Furthermore, by describing themselves as free, different and rebellious from mainstream society, some male flamenco aficionados explicitly alluded to their marginal identity (Matteucci, 2014).

Another allusion to the construction of gendered, marginal identities is made by Menet (2020) in the tourist experience of salsa dancing. She refers to Patric, one male research participant, who describes masculinity in salsa as 'macho-like', which intimates that the 'constructions of gender in salsa also intersect with specific representations of "Latinness"' (p. 106). Although salsa, flamenco, and many other forms of intangible heritage have become transnational phenomena, the construction of identities remains something highly subjective and personal, yet shaped by collective cultural myths. In his ethnographic work in multiple locations, Skinner (2007) observes that while the practice of salsa provides Latin Americans an occasion to express and confirm their cultural identity, for the Germans in the salsa class the practice 'takes them away from their home, from their everyday: it is their time for fantasy, escapism, and difference; and the salsa dancing is an ability or skill learned and honed through discipline, practice and diligence' (p. 492). Like for the flamenco tourists, Skinner notes, the Latin Americans embrace the struggles or narratives of resistance and oppression communicated within the music.

5.1.2 Cultural and Cosmopolitan Identities

Participation in serious leisure activities, to which creative tourism belongs – however away from home – has been seen as a way through which people can reaffirm their cultural identities. The example of the salsa dance classes, as informed by Skinner (2007), emphasises this link. Different cultural groups have different relationships with music, for instance. Skinner notes that, for Latin Americans living in Europe, engaging in salsa allows them to reconnect with their roots, whether these dancers are from Colombia, Cuba or any other Latin American country. Because these salsa aficionados belong to the Latin American diaspora, reconnecting with their homeland is particularly important to them. Bizas (2014) similarly asserts that for some Afro-Americans, drumming and dancing Sabar is a tool to celebrate their cultural (African) identity. Another example of creative tourism as a metaphor of cultural identity affirmation is provided by Creighton (1995). In the mountains of Shinshū, a remote area of the Japan Alps, Creighton accounts for the creative tourist experiences of affluent Japanese women who attend a week-long silk-weaving workshop. Creighton presents the context of the silk-weaving holiday as follows:

> [T]he vacationing women live communally, cooperatively clean and maintain the premises, and take turns in cooking meals for the group. They learn to weave silk on large looms that require coordinated arm and leg movements. However, the women do not just learn how to weave silk. They are required to learn and experience what the instructors consider the entire traditional silk-weaving process. They tend silk-worms, boil silk cocoons and process the batting, spin their own silk threads, and go out into the mountains to collect grasses and other natural materials from which they dye the spun threads into various colors. Each workshop day begins at 6:00 a.m. as the women prepare to exercise together to the nationally broadcast *rajio taisō* (radio exercises). However, most participants are awake at 5:00 a.m., cleaning rooms or assisting with breakfast preparations. The women are in group classes, or working on their own projects throughout the day and into the late hours of the evening, usually retiring close to midnight. (p. 465)

These craft holidays, Creighton notes, are situated within the increasing westernisation of Japanese daily lifestyles and 'the extensive promotion of nostalgia and tradition' by the Japanese tourism industry (p. 465). Nostalgia is metaphorically represented in images of Japan's mountains and rurality as well as in silk-weaving, an ancestral and traditional Japanese folk-craft. Not only mountainous areas are thought to epitomise the traditional Japanese lifestyle of the past, but silk-weaving is also commonly associated with the past domestic labour of Japanese married women. For these female urban dwellers, learning silk-weaving, according to Creighton, 'is itself part of the nostalgic journey to reunion with a Japanese self' (p. 468).

Creighton, who draws from various Japanese scholars, remarks that in the Japanese society, social activities such as leisure pursuits and travel are typically 'homosocial', which means that activities involving members of the same sex tend to be the social norm. Furthermore, involvement in handicrafts – handicrafts being largely imbued with female gender roles – enables women to experience enjoyment and empowerment or to gain a sense of control over their bodies. However, the stories told by the creative female tourists transcend a sense of fulfilment experienced in doing handicrafts. Likewise, while the Japanese women's participation in silk-weaving workshops is situated within a nostalgic search for the Japanese self, Creighton notes that cultural identity is also closely related to the construction of gendered identities. She suggests that

> [w]hereas before these [silk-weaving activities] were domains of women's work, under the control of men; now these were experienced by the women as domains of women's work, which they themselves controlled [...] The women were not trying to enhance female status by entering the 'male realm' or activities more commonly assigned to men in Japanese society. Instead, the women were attempting to recapture female realms of activities, and gain control of them. (pp. 475–476)

What the Japanese women's participation in silk-weaving workshops has revealed is that not only the creative tourist experience represents a search for cultural identity, but it also serves as a metaphor of female agency. Other authors, albeit not in the creative tourism context, have similarly reported the agentic power of shared holiday experiences among women (e.g. Jordan & Gibson, 2005; Matteucci, 2022b). Another type of identity enhancement enacted through creative experiences is the construction of a cosmopolitan identity.

Cosmopolitans are mobile urbanites who are interested in divergent cultural experiences and have acquired some knowledge and skills with foreign cultures (Hannerz, 1992). Being a cosmopolitan means being open to the world. In fact, in ancient Greek, *kosmos* means universe and *polis* means city, which means that a cosmopolitan is a global citizen (Salazar, 2010). Because tourism is a global phenomenon, it is 'potentially both a cosmopolitan-making and a worldmaking industry' (Swain, 2009, p. 507). However, all tourists are not necessarily cosmopolitan (Hannerz, 2004) because many of them, like Cohen's recreational and diversionary types of tourists, are either looking for home abroad or for places where they can recover from their daily routine. Yet, as we have seen throughout this book, despite their heterogeneity, creative tourists perform a kind of cosmopolitanism that can 'promote competencies to negotiate, translate other countries and cultures from consumerism to learning and practice' (Swain, 2009, p. 521). In other words, creative tourists cosmopolitanise through immersive experiences learning from and with hosts about their endogenous cultural heritage(s).

Examples of cosmopolitan identities are found in culinary tourists through the deployment of savoir-faire, namely a cultural skill set how to consume heritage, goods and places. Beyond a repertoire of new recipes and authentic embodied experiences of Thai cuisine, what the Thai cooking schools offer to tourists, Mills (2019) asserts, are opportunities 'to tell themselves about themselves' (p. 53). Mills clarifies that what is at stake in the playful cooking classes 'is not really a story about Thai cultural or culinary heritage. Rather, it is a story about hierarchies of value and cosmopolitan identities, a story about whose appetites for authenticity count on the global stage' (p. 53). Some tourists seek to fulfil their desire of difference through performing imagined identities through cooking classes. Others, such as the creative tourists in Menet's (2020) ethnographic study, imagined their cosmopolitan lifestyle as salsa dancers in their countries of origin. For some dancers, what a cosmopolitan lifestyle evokes is an opportunity to sustain a career in the European salsa circuit. Here, the cosmopolitan tourists' imaginary is filled with ideas of openness to new social encounters and with the travel opportunities that these encounters may engender.

While modernity may have spawned many homogeneous urban centres, difference and diversity are still to be found in the nooks and crannies of these centres, in serendipitous encounters with singular personalities, and in the climate and geography that mark people and places. Perhaps, we should understand the enactment of cosmopolitan identities as a desire to grasp alterity through instinctive impulses in immersive, vivid performances. The creative tourist could be said to be, therefore, both an artist and a cosmopolitan nomad. When Onfray (2007) presents the cosmopolitan traveller as a 'nomade-artiste' (a nomadic artist), he alludes to the acute sensitivity and the entangled subjectivities that pertain to the creative tourist's experience. As some scholars have argued (e.g. Hannerz, 2004), a core quality of cosmopolitanism is to be open to the world. To be open as a 'nomade-artiste', Onfray asserts, means to 'primarily celebrate that which makes us shiver and become electrified, move and be charged with energy' (p. 67). With this state of mind, this openness to the world, the creative tourist is likely to find herself/himself confronted to herself/himself. In other words, travelling as a creative tourist opens up the possibility to negotiate one's own subjective self (Onfray, 2007).

5.2 Inspiration and Self-transformation

Earlier, we concluded Chapter 4 by arguing that creative tourist spaces possess the agency to foster positive emotions and, in turn, to promote positive change in those who dwell in them. In the first half of this chapter, we have also demonstrated that creative tourism affords opportunities to create and affirm identities. Informed by Foucault's theorisation of heterotopia, we have argued, as Topinka (2010) put it, that heterogeneous creative tourism environments are 'spatial organs of knowledge production' (p. 66). The key proponent of serious leisure, Robert Stebbins (1982) has similarly presented creative forms of cultural tourism as sites for 'self-actualization, self-enrichment, re-creation or renewal of self, feelings of accomplishment, enhancement of self-image, self-expression, social interaction and belongingness' (p. 252). Here, we will highlight the inspirational and transformational potential of the creative tourist experience.

It has become commonplace to emphasise the link between travel and self-development. Many authors have written about the personal benefits of travel, from Stoic Roman philosopher Seneca to French novelist Marcel Proust (1871–1922). Henry Miller's (1957) famous quote, which says '[o]ne's destination is never a place, but rather a new way of looking at things' (p. 25), is one among many other examples that boasts the eye-opening power of travel. For instance, many of the cosmopolitan tourists' testimonies available on the VAWAA platform suggest that, through creative practices, tourists not only acquire the knowledge and skills that nourish their quest for cultural capital, but they also find some inspiration to pursue creative activities back home. Bettina, an Australian tourist who followed a five-day Ebru painting course in Istanbul, expressed her journey in the following terms:

> During my residency I had the opportunity to learn and practice Turkish Marbling thoroughly, as well as gaining important understanding of the mysticism and philosophy which surround this ancient art form. I will definitely incorporate the newfound knowledge in my practice, in fact it will probably send me on a different path. I am very grateful for what I have learned and experienced.

Another Australian tourist commented on the traditional shadow puppetry workshop that she took in Malaysia: '[t]here is no doubt the skills, knowledge and inspiration from this week will influence my personal creative practice and curiosity. I'm looking forward to seeing where it goes!'. These two creative experiences are not talked about in terms of a deep personal transformation per se, but in terms of an invigorating and inspirational thrust. In their study with working artists in the Ouseburn Valley area of Newcastle upon Tyne, England, Whiting and Hannam (2014) similarly found that the artists' sojourns to other places were reminiscent of the practices of artists from the Romantic Movement in that these acted 'as sources of romanticised "inspiration"' (p. 73). The creative experience holds significant aesthetic-reflexive meanings for the tourists (Whiting & Hannam, 2014) and it clearly gives tourists a fresh impetus for further artistic exploration upon their return. Holistic retreats increasingly focus on creative pursuits (e.g. dancing, singing, music, painting) in addition to spiritual ones (e.g. yoga, meditation) with the overall aim of facilitating transformation as well as providing rest, relaxation and escapism. In her discourse analysis of retreats, Smith (2023) notes the frequent employment of terms relating to eudaimonic personal growth and development, for example, 'to improve', 'to enhance', 'to cultivate', 'to learn', 'to become'. Ultimately, the discourse revolves around a process of supported personal development that allows the participant to return to a life of 'becoming', which involves individual growth and betterment. The power of the creative tourist experience goes far beyond the tourist-host encounter. It also transcends the tourists themselves as illustrated in the following excerpt from Kim Marie, a Vietnamese creative tourist who learned about traditional dyeing and weaving techniques in Vietnam:

> From the turning of soil, to the sewing of seeds, harvesting of indigo, to weaving/dyeing of fabric, processing of cotton and living in a world where buffalo play and colour emerges [...] the course has not only supported my personal creative journey in the

most extraordinary and immersive way but allowed me to visualise how I can encourage young people to learn from our heritage and make life choices that will support a more sustainable future.

The words articulated above intimate the creative tourist experience as 'an array of intensities' (Deleuze, 1990, p. 156) or an event that possesses agency to foster relational goods. A teacher in Hanoi, Kim Marie, who has been deeply impacted by her creative experience, here asserts her sincere commitment to 'inspire' her own students 'to become the ethical designers of tomorrow'. Her words connote an affirmative ethics of care, a form of political activism, which unambiguously stems from the immersive and collaborative practices pertaining to the creative tourist experience. Kim Marie's commitment to what appears to be ethically transformative echoes the happiness concept of *social eudaimonia* (Onfray, 2008), which foregrounds collective rather than individual well-being.

While the inspirational and personal growth potential of creative tourism has been ascertained, so far the scholarly literature has offered little empirical evidence of the transformational power of creative tourism on the tourist. Like all social phenomena, tourist transformation is a process, which could be metaphorically represented as a volcanic eruption or a process of decantation as exposed by Onfray (2007) in the following excerpt:

> One experiences confusion and a hodgepodge of feelings, then the incoherence of perceptions. The pleasure inflicts its jolts in the middle of the chaos of information registered by a body that has worked at full speed. After experiencing enchantment, the feast of reality, traveling back home muddles the waters and calls for a full decantation process. The cluttered, heavy, charged skies, then swept away by the breath of the soul, fade away in favour of a washed ether, clear and limpid. In the fatigue felt upon returning home, the syntheses to come are being brewed. (Original in French below – translated by the authors.)

> [On expérimente la confusion et le mélange des sensations, puis l'incohérence des perceptions. La jouissance inflige ses soubresauts au beau milieu du capharnaüm d'informations engrangées par un corps ayant fonctionné à plein régime. Après la féerie de l'évènement, la fête du réel, le retour trouble les eaux et appelle une réelle décantation. Les ciels encombrés, lourds, chargés, puis balayés par le souffle de l'esprit s'effacent au profit d'un éther lavé, limpide et clair. Dans la fatigue du retour se préparent les synthèses à venir.] (pp. 101–102)

Tourist transformation is obviously not systematic and tourists may feel changed to very different degrees depending on many factors (Kirilova et al., 2017; Sheldon, 2020). However, what is common to many studies of tourist transformative experiences is the intensity of the emotions experienced, the regenerative and soothing power of nature, the perceived authenticity of the spaces inhabited, immersive participation, as well as the socialisation opportunities that are conducive to feelings of togetherness or communitas. Holistic and creative retreat discourse encapsulates the realisation of human potential, personal growth, development and fulfilment in supportive and collective spaces. Such spaces provide meaningful and authentic experiences that foster altruism and nature-(re)connection and help to create universal harmony (Smith, 2023). These transformative forms of tourism relate to an initiation or a rite of passage (Van Gennep, 1909; Turner, 1969), which is characterised by three transitory phases: the phase of separation where the tourist leaves her/his usual environment, the phase of liminality (transition between two spaces), and the phase of incorporation, which implies a return home, a reintegration within the environment of departure.

For travel, this transitional phase is both a space-time and a physical space that separates the tourist from home. In this phase, the traveller adapts to the destination's environment, thus gradually setting aside the norms and conventions of her/his home environment and adopting a new 'tourist' lifestyle characterised by unbridled behaviour commensurate with the traveller's imagination and what is tolerated within the space visited (Jafari, 1987). The phase of liminality (or liminoidity) is thus similar to a kind of intoxication that fades or disappears once the traveller returns to her/his place of residence. Several studies have focused on the so-called 'fade-out' effect of tourist experiences, which involves a decline of positive emotions on return home. However, for the longest journeys, Jafari (1987) expects a more intense shock during the reintegration phase. The rite of passage, therefore, has the power to mark in one way or another the identity project of the person who experiences it.

To illustrate this marker in one's life or creative tourist transformative experiences, we draw from different accounts. The first account comes from Ainhoa, a creative tourist who spent five days in Cao Bang, an artisanal village north of Hanoi, in order to learn the traditional Vietnamese indigo dyeing process. In the backdrop of her creative experience, Ainhoa discloses the need she felt for finding some relief from her stressful everyday life:

> I had the concern to do some artistic matter which helps me to destress and to surface my creative capacity, calming my out and insider rhythm of living. I also had long since needed a trip to an exotic and distant place [...] It has given me the energy, ideas and strength I needed at this vital moment.

While not all tourists search in creative activities a release from their everyday tensions, what is clear in the data presented here is that transformative experiences are simply not the mere result of on-site stimuli, rather of a complex process of maturation; a process that may have started long before the trip (Matteucci, 2022a). In this process the body registers sensations, filters information, manages tensions, pain and suffering (Onfray, 1991), which build up and then germinate until these hatch. It is important to remember that eudaimonic approaches to well-being are engendered not only by pleasurable experiences, but also by challenging and sometimes painful ones (Knobloch, Roberston, & Aitken, 2017). Here, Ainhoa's experience corresponds to a rejuvenating episode that allows her to recalibrate and start afresh. In the same vein, Natalie expresses her malaise before her creative trip to Spain:

> I mean for my work back there [in Canada], she had to hire a contractor who probably cost more than I do to cover me for those six months that I took off. You work for 5 years and you can take six months off and not get fired [laugh]. 'Cause you're either burnt out and quit or you take a sabbatical, so I've chosen a sabbatical. [...] With me I think I was ... I was always trying to be that person that everybody expects me to be, and it was just easier to do things like to focus on other people instead of myself. [...] You know. I've been in a relationship for 15 years solid, so, so it's just never been about me ... I think that's the whole catholic upbringing too [laugh] ... I've never really realized how strong it was until I was traveling. Just the whole idea of self-sacrifice and you know, pride being a negative thing, vanity being a negative thing, like all those you need to be a strong person ... Well, I've learnt a ridiculous amount about myself, things I didn't know were there and so I know when I go home there's gonna be some significant changes that not everybody is gonna be happy about. (Matteucci, 2012, p. 246)

This quotation evokes the disintegration of Natalie's emotional life and the challenge to her value system. Fifteen years of a deteriorating sentimental relationship have left their mark on her flesh and soul, and here Natalie speaks of her resignation, self-sacrifice, alluding to her blindness during those years. She became aware of the shackles that hindered her personal development, namely the Judeo-Christian straitjacket that prescribes self-denial and feelings of guilt. The burn out that Natalie alluded to during our conversation points to the human biological need to regain balance, which corresponds to a process of self-reappropriation. The hardship that she had gone through traced the path towards a pivotal moment in her life. This pivotal moment is sometimes invested with vivid emotions, acute bodily sensations, a kind of transcendental state as exemplified in the following quote from Laura, extracted from Matteucci (2018), who talks about the emotional discharge felt during a dance exam at her flamenco school:

> It was definitely a strong moment because I told many people about it ... It was the first time in my life that I totally felt myself into it ... Now I understand what it means to give the best of yourself, like you forget that they're people around you ... I don't know, what I was telling my parents is that I don't know what happened to me there. I think I've just really thrown myself into it and when you feel something that others also tell you that they have felt it, there is this satisfaction that, maybe, there is a chance that you can understand ... In fact, I've started to understand what flamenco is about ... I forgot that this was an exam, 'cause usually in exams

you feel stress. But there, I forgot about it, just like if I were on my own. That was weird, like if I had smoked [pot]. I was fully into it. Yeah, I was into that song ... like there is this feeling of warmth that takes you, actually like if all the emotions in your whole body were coming out. I was even shivering, really! (p. 14)

For Laura, the dance exam represents a culminating liminoid experience akin to a catharsis or a transcendental experience. While dancing Laura embodies the emotions transported by the song and she forgets the world around her. In his analysis of flow as an optimal experience, Csikszentmihalyi (1990) uses the term *autotelic* to describe this ineffable, extremely rewarding experience during which the body, mind and environment become one. This event fills Laura with joy, with some positive regenerative energy. It is a pivotal moment in her life trajectory in that it 'breaks with the anxiety and groping of the past allowing a liberation of her body and mind' (Matteucci, 2018, p. 12). For many creative tourists, like Natalie and Laura in Spain, and Ainhoa in Vietnam, the creative tourist experience is revealed as therapeutic. The regenerative nature of the creative experience is unambiguously articulated by Aglaé when she says:

Actually, for me, flamenco is like a sort of therapy ... because I didn't have a clear goal in life. I was studying something I didn't like, so it was like a way to let out all the things that I had inside, all the emotions ... (Matteucci, 2012, p. 241)

A vast range of transformative experiences have been documented in the tourism literature from mild transformations (e.g. Pung et al., 2020) to cathartic experiences (e.g. Matteucci, 2018; Zahra & McIntosh, 2007). What is common to all cathartic experiences is the state of tranquility, serenity or peace of mind that one undergoes after an emotional climax. This state of tranquility is known as ataraxia. Ataraxia thus corresponds to a release from anxiety or an embodied liberation, which is prone to reflection (Onfray, 1991). Informed by Onfray, Matteucci (2022b) metaphorically presents ataraxia as '[t]he calmness felt after a storm or the regenerative aftermath of a volcanic eruption' (p. 633). It is worth noting that, contrary to Aristotelian philosophy, which equates happiness with human flourishing, in Epicurean philosophy, happiness or eudaimonia entails the attainment of ataraxia (Massie, 2018). While learning and self-development have been abundantly emphasised in the creative tourism literature, an Epicurean philosophy of happiness suggests that happiness is perhaps not so much about flourishing but more about liberating oneself from the pressures and shackles of modern capitalist societies. In fact, Massie (2018) argues that 'to reach ataraxia is to raise oneself above a condition of misery and despair' (p. 384). For instance, his attempt at liberating himself from his past 'yobbish' life is unequivocally expressed by Peter, a 29-year old Welsh creative tourist who followed a two-week flamenco guitar course in Seville:

[I came here] to learn to like myself and to better myself, learn to forget the bad things in the past and start a new chapter. You know.

> Yeah, it's a self bettering experience. As I said, I use the guitar as a form of meditation. 'Cause at that time I'm in my purist bliss [...] When I'm playing guitar there is no demons nagging my head, you know ... I'm trying to get rid of my scars, you know, try to patch up my scars [...] This is why I feel I'm blessed because I've broken the chains of people saying 'you can't do this, you can't do that, you can't do this'. You gotta be a rebel as well. I am a rebel. But it is a good thing. A little bit a rebellion is good. (Matteucci, 2012, pp. 175 & 241)

As Peter's account suggests, the tourist transformation process is situated within a eudaimonic pursuit; a pursuit that aims at living a more meaningful life. By describing his behaviour as rebellious, Peter intimates the creative tourist experience as a space of resistance or heterotopia (Foucault, 1986). Through the various tourists' accounts presented here, the connectivity of systems, so dear to Deleuze and Guattari (1980), has been established. Therefore, any serious attempt at exploring the subtleties underlying tourist transformations calls for attending to creative tourists' life trajectories, namely their past and current struggles, their affective relations and practices. Following Deleuze's vocabulary, we construe the transformative experience as a significant process of *deterritorialisation* and then *reterritorialisation* of the tourist. In other words, for cathartic experiences, as Matteucci (2022b) argues, the creative tourist transformation consists of 'a liberating rupture followed by a realignment of emotions and sensualities allowing a profound reordering of the being' (p. 634).

References

Aramberri, J. (2001). The host should get lost. Paradigms in the tourist theory. *Annals of Tourism Research, 28*(3), 738–761. doi:10.1016/S0160-7383(00)00075-X

Bauman, Z. (2000). *Liquid modernity*. Cambridge: Polity Press.

Bizas, E. (2014). *Learning Senegalese Sabar: Dancers and embodiment in New York and Dakar*. London: Berghahn Books.

Boorstin, D. J. (1964). *The Image: A guide to pseudo-events in America*. New York, NY: Harper & Row.

Brown, L. (2013). Tourism: A catalyst for existential authenticity. *Annals of Tourism Research, 40*, 176–190. doi:10.1016/j.annals.2012.08.004

Cloninger, R. C. (2004). *Feeling good: The science of well-being*. Oxford: Oxford University Press.

Cohen, E. (1979). A phenomenology of tourist experiences. *Journal of the British Sociological Association, 13*(2), 179–201. doi:10.1177/003803857901300203

Creighton, M. R. (1995). Japanese craft tourism: Liberating the crane wife. *Annals of Tourism Research, 22*(2), 463–478. doi:10.1016/0160-7383(94)00086-7

Csiksentmihalyi, M. (1990). *Flow: The psychology of optimal experience*. New York, NY: Harper and Row.

Deleuze, G. (1990). *Pourparlers*. Paris: Les Éditions de Minuit.

Deleuze, G., & Guattari, F. (1980). *Capitalisme et Schizophrénie 2: Mille plateaux*. Paris: Les Éditions de Minuits.

Duxbury, N., & Bakas, F. E. (2021). Creative tourism: A humanistic paradigm in practice. In M. Della Lucia & E. Giudici (Eds.), *Humanistic management and sustainable tourism: Human, social and environmental challenges* (pp. 111–131). London: Routledge.

Filep, S. (2012). Positive psychology and tourism. In M. Uysal, R. R. Perdue, & M. J. Sirgy (Eds.), *Handbook of tourism and quality-of-life research* (pp. 31–50). London: Springer.

Foucault, M. (1986). Of other spaces. *Diacritics, 16*(1), 22–27.

Fu, X., Tanyatanaboon, M., & Lehto, X. (2015). Conceptualizing transformative guest experience at retreat centers. *International Journal of Hospitality Management, 49*, 83–92. doi:10.1016/j.ijhm.2015.06.004

Gazley, A., & Watling, L. (2015). Me, my tourist self and I: The symbolic consumption of travel. *Journal of Travel & Tourism Marketing, 32*(6), 639–655. doi:10.1080/105484 08.2014.954690

Gibson, C., & Connell J. (2005). *Music and tourism, on the road again.* Clevedon, OH: Channel View Publications.

Hannerz, U. (1992). *Cultural complexity: Studies in the social organization of meaning.* Chichester: Columbia University Press.

Hannerz, U. (2004). Cosmopolitanism. In D. Nugent & J. Vincent (Eds.), *A companion to the Anthropology of Politics* (pp. 69–85). Oxford: Blackwell.

Heathwood, C. (2014). Subjectives theories of well-being. In B. Eggleston & D. Miller (Eds.) *The Cambridge companion to utilitarianism* (pp. 199–219). Cambridge: Cambridge University Press.

Heffner Hayes, M. (2009). *Flamenco: Conflicting histories of the dance.* Jefferson, NC: McFarland & Company, Inc.

Jafari, J. (1987). Tourism models: The sociocultural aspects. *Tourism Management, 8*, 151–159. doi:10.1016/0261-5177(87)90023-9

Jordan, F., & Gibson, H. (2005). "We are not stupid … but we'll not stay home either": Experiences of women solo travelers. *Tourism Review International, 9*(2), 195–211. doi:10.3727/154427205774791663

Kelly, C., & Smith, M. K. (2016). Journeys of the self: The need to retreat. In M. K. Smith & L. Puczkó (Eds.), *Routledge handbook of health tourism* (pp. 138–151). London: Routledge.

Kirillova, K., & Lehto, X. (2015). An existential conceptualization of the vacation cycle. *Annals of Tourism Research, 55*, 110–123. doi:10.1016/j.annals.2015.09.003

Kirillova, K., Lehto, X., & Cai, L. (2017). Tourism and existential transformation: An empirical investigation. *Journal of Travel Research, 56*(5), 638–650. doi:10.1177/0047287516650277

Knobloch, U., Roberston, K., & Aitken, R. (2017). Experience, emotion and eudaimonia: A consideration of tourist experiences and well-being. *Journal of Travel Research, 56*(5), 651–662. doi:10.1177/0047287516650937

Labajo, J. (2003). Body and voice: The construction of gender in flamenco. In T. Magrini (Ed.), *Music and gender: Perspectives from the Mediterranean* (pp. 67–86). Chicago, IL: University of Chicago Press.

Massie, P. (2018). Ataraxia: Tranquility at the end. In S. D. Kirkland & E. Sanday (Eds.), *A companion to ancient philosophy* (pp. 383–408). Evanston, IL: Northwestern University Press.

Matteucci, X. (2012). *The tourist experience of intangible heritage: The case of flamenco consumers.* Unpublished doctoral dissertation, Vienna University of Economics and Business (WU), Vienna.

Matteucci, X. (2014). Forms of body usage in tourists' experiences of flamenco. *Annals of Tourism Research, 46*, 29–43. doi:10.1016/j.annals.2014.02.005

Matteucci, X. (2018). Expériences touristiques, flamenco et hapax existentiel. *Leisure/ Loisir, 42*(2), 185–204. doi:10.1080/14927713.2018.1449133

Matteucci, X. (2022a). Existential hapax as tourist embodied transformation. *Tourism Recreation Research, 47*(5–6), 631–635. doi:10.1080/02508281.2021.1934330

Matteucci, X. (2022b). Female friends' holiday experiences in heterotopia. *Journal of Qualitative Research in Tourism, 3*(1), 14–31. doi:10.4337/jqrt.2022.01.02

Menet, J. (2020). *Entangled mobilities in the transnational salsa circuit: The Esperanto of the body, gender and ethnicity*. London: Routledge.

Miller, H. (1957). *Big Sur and the Oranges of Hieronymus Bosch*. New York, NY: New Directions.

Mills, M. B. (2019). Authentic dishes, staged identities: Thailand's cooking schools for tourists. *Gastronomica, 19*(2), 43–55. doi:10.1525/gfc.2019.19.2.43

Onfray, M. (1991). *L'Art de jouir. Pour un matérialisme hédoniste*. Paris: Grasset.

Onfray, M. (2007). *Théorie du voyage: Poétique de la géographie*. Paris: Grasset.

Onfray, M. (2008). *L'eudémonisme social. Contre-histoire de la philosophie V*. Paris: Grasset.

Pung, J. M., Yung, R., Khoo-Lattimore, C., & Del Chiappa, G. (2020). Transformative travel experiences and gender: A double duoethnography approach. *Current Issues in Tourism, 23*(5), 538–558. doi:10.1080/13683500.2019.1635091

Reisinger, Y. (2013). *Transformational tourism: Tourist perspectives*. Wallingford: CABI.

Rosaldo, R. (1989). *Culture and truth: The remaking of social analysis*. London: Routledge.

Ross, S. L. (2020). A concept analysis of the properties and conditions of transformation. *Advances in Social Sciences Research Journal, 7*(5), 522–544. doi:10.14738/assrj.75.8344

Ryan, R. M., & Deci, E. L. (2000). Self-determination theory and the facilitation of intrinsic motivation, social development and wellbeing. *American Psychologist, 55*, 68–78. doi:10.1037/0003-066X.55.1.68

Salazar, N. B. (2010). Tourism and cosmopolitanism: A view from below. *International Journal of Tourism Anthropology, 1*(1), 55–69. doi:10.1504/IJTA.2010.036846

Sheldon, P. (2020). Designing tourism experiences for inner transformation. *Annals of Tourism Research, 83*, 102935. doi:10.1016/j.annals.2020.102935

Sirgy, M. J., & Su, C. (2000). Destination image, self-congruity, and travel behavior: Toward an integrative model. *Journal of Travel Research, 38*(4), 340–352. doi:10.1177/004728750003800402

Skinner, J. (2007). The salsa class: A complexity of globalization, cosmopolitans and emotions. *Identities: Global Studies in Culture and Power, 14*, 485–506. doi:10.1080/10702890701578480

Smith, M. K. (2013). Wellness tourism and its transformational practices. In Y. Reisinger (Ed.), *Transformational tourism tourist perspectives* (pp. 55–67). Wallingford: CABI.

Smith, M. K. (2023). Retreating towards subjective well-being. In T. V. Singh, R. Butler, & D. A. Fennell (Eds.), *Tourism as a pathway to hope and happiness* (pp. 135–151). Bristol: Channel View.

Smith, M. K., & Diekmann, A. (2017). Tourism and wellbeing. *Annals of Tourism Research, 66*, 1–13. doi:10.1016/j.annals.2017.05.006

Sørensen, A. D. (2010). *Philosophy and therapy of existence: Perspectives in existential analysis*. Aarhus: The State and University Library in Aarhus.

Stebbins, R. A. (1982). Serious leisure: A conceptual statement. *Pacific Sociological Review, 25*(2), 251–272. doi:10.2307/1388726

Swain, M. B. (2009). The Cosmopolitan hope of tourism: Critical action and worldmaking vistas. *Tourism Geographies, 11*(4), 505–525. doi:10.1080/14616680903262695

Theodossopoulos, D. (2012). Dance, visibility and representational self-awareness in an Emberá community in Panama. In H. Neveu Kringelbach & J. Skinner (Eds.), *Dancing cultures: Globalization, tourism and identity in the anthropology of dance* (pp. 121–140). Oxford: Berghahn.

Topinka, R. J. (2010). Foucault, Borges, heterotopia: Producing knowledge in other spaces. *Foucault Studies, 9*, 54–70. doi:10.22439/fs.v0i9.3059

Turner, V. (1969). *The ritual process: Structure and anti-structure*. New Brunswick, NJ: Aldine De Gruyter.

Urbain, J.-D. (2002). *L'idiot du Voyage: Histoires de Touristes* (2nd ed.). Paris: Éditions Payot et Rivages.

Urbain, J.-D. (2007). Le touriste: Du sujet symptôme à l'homme qui rêve. *Synergies pays Riverains de la Baltique, 4*, 15–25.

Van Gennep, A. (1909). *Les rites de passage, étude systématique des rites de la porte et du seuil, de l'hospitalité, de l'adoption, de la grossesse et de l'accouchement, de la naissance, de l'enfance, de la puberté, de l'initiation, de l'ordination, du couronnement, des fiançailles et du mariage, des funérailles, des saisons, etc.* Librairie Critique Émile Nourry [réimp. Mouton et Maison des Sciences de l'Homme 1969].

Wearing, S., Stevenson, D., & Young, T. (2010). *Tourist cultures: Identity, place and the traveller*. London: Sage.

Whiting, J., & Hannam, K. (2014). Journeys of inspiration: Working artists' reflections on tourism. *Annals of Tourism Research, 49*, 65–75. doi:10.1016/j.annals.2014.08.007

Zahra, A., & McIntosh, A. J. (2007). Volunteer tourism: Evidence of cathartic tourist experiences. *Tourism Recreation Research, 32*(1), 115–119. doi:10.1080/02508281.2007.11081530

Chapter 6

Synthesis and Reflections

The creative tourist experience is dynamic, multifaceted and potentially trans-formative. In creative tourism, individuals interact with endogenous tangible and intangible heritage with the primary objective to expand their knowledge and develop some skills. Contrary to some commentators (e.g. Duxbury & Richards, 2019) who accept that creative tourism does not always include immersive, artistic practices, we believe that what makes creative tourism different from other forms of tourism and intrinsically valuable for both tourists and communities is pre-cisely the integration of creative artistic practices and the tangible and intangible characteristics of place. What we have sought to demonstrate in this book is that creative tourists not only engage in place-specific resources for self-fulfilment purposes but they also seek to nurture and negotiate their own embodied identities. This quest is in itself a joyful creative process. Immersive, active and sensuous engagement in heterogenous spaces is a central feature of the creative tourist experience. Informed by a Deleuzian reading of space which underscores the relational (or rhizomatic) and fluid nature of the world, we have presented the creative tourist experience as a sociocultural, permeable space in which people play, enact new role identities and cultivate self-awareness. While creative tourist environments can be more or less contrived and regulated, we have demonstrated that heterogenous creative tourist spaces are prone to stimulate stronger emo-tions than regulated commercial environments and offer imaginative and enacted alternatives to normative everyday spaces. We have characterised creative tourist spaces as liminoid for their playful and transitional nature and as heterotopic for their disruptive capacity to affect those who dwell in them. In addition, we have argued that a sense of authenticity and intimacy are inherent qualities of heterogenous, creative tourist spaces. Experiences of existential authenticity and the intimate socialities of some creative tourist spaces are conducive to enhanced well-being through empowerment, bonding and self-transformation.

While we do not dismiss the relevance of escapism and hedonistic pleasures underlying participation in creative tourism, the creative tourist experience is essen-tially revealed as eudaimonic in character. Indeed, in many studies of creative tour-ism, the core motives underpinning creative tourist experiences, as illustrated in this book, point to the central pursuit of personal expressiveness (Waterman, 1993) or eudaimonia. In Aristotelian philosophy, a eudaimonic person is a virtuous person;

The Creative Tourist: A Eudaimonic Perspective, 87–96

Copyright © 2024 by Xavier Matteucci and Melanie Kay Smith

Published under exclusive licence by Emerald Publishing Limited

doi:10.1108/978-1-83753-404-320241006

that is a person who engages in good actions for his/her own self and for others (Pearce, Filep, & Ross, 2011). Moreover, research in positive psychology has confirmed that pursuing excellence gives meaning and direction to one's life (Waterman, 1993). If travel, in its widest sense, is nothing less than a pursuit of happiness (Urbain, 2007), participation in creative tourism can also be said to correspond to a deeper search for meaning (Agrawal & Pato de Carvalho, 2021). Not only does living a meaningful life contribute to the well-being of the individual, but also, as Pearce et al. (2011) assert, 'to the well-being of the wider world around the person' (p. 84). This point connects strongly to the recent positioning of creative tourism as a regenerative form of tourism that create positive outcomes for destinations and communities (Duxbury, Bakas, Vinagre de Castro, & Silva, 2021). This observation also suggests that creative tourism may lead the way towards greater collective well-being; an important point that we will return to below. However, to stay at the individual level, we are joining a chorus of theorists, such as Albert Camus (1913–1960), who recognise the intrinsic value of artistic creation as a means through which individuals strive to make their life a work of art.

In *L'Homme Révolté* (The Rebel) first published in 1951, Camus posits that man is alienated by an oppressive elite, a tortured man who, through artistic creativity, endlessly seeks to give form to his life. Camus (1951, 1982) argues that

> man has an idea of a better world than [his everyday life]. But better does not mean different, it means unified. This passion which lifts the mind above the commonplaces of a dispersed world, from which it nevertheless detaches itself, is this passion for unity. (p. 228)

This 'idea of a better world', as Camus says, is 'an imaginary world [...] which is created from the rectification of the actual world' (p. 229). Through creative pursuits '[m]an is finally able to give himself the alleviating form and limits which he pursues in vain in his own life' (p. 229). The passions alluded to by Camus are manifested in creative tourism activities like flamenco, salsa and sabar dance and music. Indeed, as Duxbury, Pato de Carvalho, and Albino (2021) remark, 'creative tourism activities are linked to personal passions and pursuits, with travel being an extension of these interests' (p. 7). If creative tourists draw from their passions to engage in activities that give meaning to their lives, it seems coherent to view creative tourist practices as acts of resistance, hence our argument that the creative tourist space may be comprehended as a heterotopia (Foucault, 1986). In fact, Deleuze (1988) has similarly articulated the act of creation as an act of resistance. Deleuze maintains that by engaging in artistic creation women and men are able to liberate life that they have imprisoned. They are able to liberate a powerful life (une vie puissante), a life that transcends the self. Deleuze (1990) cites art historian Alois Riegl (1858–1905) who postulates that the three functions of art are to beautify nature, to spiritualise nature and to compete with nature. We believe that the first two functions are relevant to our discussion on the creative tourist. Creative tourists may not seek to beautify nature as such; however, they are concerned with the construction of their embodied self (hence to beautify the self), and their quest for creativity may be akin to a spiritual journey (Matteucci, 2013). Creative tourists' pursuits can sometimes resemble those of many yoga tourists undertaking physical pilgrimages through travel (e.g. to India); journeys that McCartney (2020) describes as 'metaphysical' (p. 98). Following Camus and Deleuze's lines of thought, a central concern of the creative tourist, we argue, is therefore to invent new modes of existence for oneself. In other words, for creative tourists, as *nomade-artistes* (Onfray, 2007), exploring new possibilities of life constitutes an attempt at a unified self, a free and (becoming) authentic self.

6.1 Future Research on Creative Tourist Experiences

The creative tourist experiences presented in this book include, among others, cooking classes in Russia, Thailand and Indonesia, silk-weaving classes in Japan, batá drumming classes in Cuba, salsa dance classes in Cuba, flamenco dance and music classes in Andalusia, sabar dance classes in Senegal and harvesting and wine-making in Portugal. While many studies of creative tourism can be found, very few offer an in-depth analysis of the creative tourist experience. Furthermore, many studies of creative tourists do not employ the 'creative tourism' label as a framework, which makes it challenging to locate this work. As the reader may have noticed, much focus has been placed on cooking and dance and music classes, making room for explorations of many other creative tourism activities. In our literature search for empirical examinations of creative tourist experiences, we were surprised that no creative tourism studies were conducted on circus and aerial arts, bread making, olive oil making, honey making, perfume making, archaeological excavation and a host of handicraft activities such as basket weaving, soap making, calligraphy, rug making, tapestry, knitting, quilting, leather crafting and glassblowing. Handicraft production relies on local knowledge, tends to be small-scale and it has traditionally satisfied the needs of local economies. Given the enormous opportunities that handicraft provides for locals and tourists to come together and create shared social capital that would invigorate communities (Scherf, 2021), this lack of attention to endogenous handicraft is regrettable. There is, therefore, scope for creative tourist studies to focus on a multiplicity of handicraft activities such as the ones enumerated above.

If creative tourism relates to personal passions pursued away from home (Duxbury, Pato de Carvalho, & Albino, 2021), we wonder how important the actual place and host community are for creative tourists compared to practicing their art in their leisure time back home? In other words, is it the promise of authentic interactions with local hosts and their culture that differentiates creative tourism from creative leisure? Further exploration of the role of place, local artisans and artists as well as experiences of authenticity would shed light on the relational power of creative tourism. In the creative tourist experience, not only the local hosts occupy a central position but also fellow tourists play a key role. As we have shown in this book, an essential dimension of the creative tourist experience is linked to social encounters and a sense of intimacy. Thus, creative tourism has been portrayed as a salient facilitator of friendship (Matteucci, 2018; Windress, 2016), a sense of belonging to a community united through passion (Menet, 2020; Törnqvist, 2018) or communitas (Matteucci & Filep, 2017). Further research may examine the type of friendship and relationships developed in the creative tourist space. Closely connected to friendship is the concept of love which, to a lesser extent, has also emerged from studies of creative tourist experiences. As evidenced in studies of dance tourism (e.g. Bizas, 2014; Menet, 2020), love can take various forms such as loving the dance form, loving dancing or falling in love with aficionados whether these are fellow students or local instructors. Furthermore, the prospect of feeling love or finding love through creative tourism may be scrutinised. Thus, it would be worth exploring how creative tourists negotiate their mobilities in the intimate sphere of romantic relationships. Like friendship, love is a fluid, complex and multidimensional concept (Filep & Matteucci, 2020) that has received little attention in creative tourist studies.

We have noted the gap in creative tourism studies connected to embodiment. Acknowledging the entanglement of multiple elements in the creative tourist experience calls for explorations of how minds and moving bodies encounter other bodies, objects and materialities. For instance, Prince (2017) notes that issues relating to touch for a creative practitioner can sometimes actually act as a barrier to interaction with tourists or sales of creative products due to sticky hands (e.g. clay when making pottery) or working with dangerous substances (e.g. hot glass). For such explorations, researchers could draw from the notion of *creative embodiment* (Richard, Glaveanu, & Aubertin, 2022) or more specifically from the *4 E* approach (Malinin, 2019) to creativity. The 4 E approach entails the interplay of body-mind (embodied) in various spaces (embedded), with relevant objects (extended), which are acted upon in meaningful ways (enactive). Malinin (2019) argues that collaborative processes afford more potential for research on creativity than cognitive processes alone. Following a new materialist perspective, which involves attending to assemblages, the entanglements of human and non-human bodies, affective relations and practices, we may come to a more nuanced understanding of the complex unfolding of creative tourist experiences. Fullagar (2017) suggests to explore the 'intra-active relations that produce different ways of feeling' (p. 253). Intra-active relations are impersonal and trans-individual forces encountered between individuals that represent 'a potential of experience' (Kumm & Pate, 2023, p. 4). Inspired by Deleuzian philosophy, Massumi (1995) refers to these intensities as *affect*. Affect is the conditional mode of an emotion. It is also what makes the intensity of an emotion. Because affect is what makes an emotion exist as a potential, because it is invisible, it is difficult to capture and articulate. For instance, Natalie, an American creative tourist who took a five-day course of traditional Turkish paper marbling in Istanbul, finds it difficult to describe her teacher's aura: 'My experience during my VAWAA with Silvia was indescribable. She has such an amazing presence in everything she does. She was an incredible teacher in the art of marble painting and a gracious host in her home'. Likewise, Aditya, another American creative tourist who also stayed with Silvia said that she has an 'immense creative energy' and Nelly from Mauritius referred to Silvia as 'a calming presence'. These descriptions correspond to what Deleuze (1990) would refer to as an 'event' or as 'an array of intensities' (p. 156).

This magnetic field is first registered as a force by the body. The kind of vibrations that we feel with music, which then become emotions, constitute intra-active relations or intensities. Creative tourism researchers would enrich their analysis by exploring the magnetic field, the intra-relations or the intensities that produce emotional, embodied experiences. The well-rehearsed scientific techniques of mainstream academia will not suffice to shed some light on the transversal forces at play in creative tourism. In line with emergent ideas from post-qualitative inquiry (Fullagar, 2017; Lenz Taguchi, 2012; Matteucci & Gnoth, 2017; St-Pierre, Jackson, & Mazzei, 2016), we see the potential of new ways of knowing through creativity, intuition and by engaging sensually and emotionally within the creative tourism research space.

A number of commentators have perhaps too dashingly assimilated creative tourists to the Creative Class (Florida, 2002). For a more nuanced picture, it would be informative to examine the links between creative tourists and the different subgroups of the Creative Class in terms of their values and their demographic and occupational profiles. In most in-depth analyses of creative tourists' experiences, research participants are predominantly white, privileged and Western. On the other hand, Richards (2016) argued that creativity is a mobile resource that is present in all locations and layers of society; therefore it allows for more equitable participation. Nevertheless, research with non-Western subjects would contrast previous analyses. Furthermore, what is striking in most creative tourism scholarship is the lack of critical reflection in terms of issues of power relations. In this book, by taking a creative tourist perspective, we deliberately focused on what matters to the tourist; however, we are cognizant of the one-sided gaze of this direction. Korstanje, Echarri-Chavez, Cisneros-Mustelier, and George (2016) are among the few who have expressed some concerns with the way creativity has been 'reimagined as a capitalistic virtue' in order to lure consumers into 'the promise of opportunities to be creative' (p. 44). Likewise, the promise of creativity and authenticity in creative tourism has opened the doors for marketing strategies to present indigenous practices and peoples as commodities, 'subordinated to a financial dependency of periphery respecting to centre' (p. 46). Ironically, or perhaps sarcastically, Korstanje et al. (2016) see creative tourism as a fashionable idea 'to conduct more sustainable ways of exploitation' (p. 49). This viewpoint stands in contrast to Richards' (2016) suggestion that the interaction between locals and tourists is more equitable than within other forms of tourism because the skills and know-how of locals are often sought by tourist thus rendering them teachers rather than (mere) service-providers. Nevertheless, Bizas (2014) warns that in the transnational sabar scene, the idea of romance may be deployed to entice some participants to travel to West Africa, but it may also be used strategically by others (e.g. local artists). In this regard, referring to the work of locals with tourists in cooking schools in Bali, Bell (2015) asks whether what is often seen as lifestyle entrepreneurship may not be in fact 'a desperate attempt at survival' (p. 97). Thus, future studies may attend to how creative tourists' 'mobilities are both productive of and produced by unequal relations of power' (Menet, 2020, p. 23).

6.2 The Agentic Power of Creative Tourism

We would like to conclude this book with a reflection on the place of creative tourism in the face of the Anthropocene and the rise of conservative global politics. As designated by a vast number of scientists across disciplines, one of the societal challenges ahead, exacerbated by neoliberal policies, is the predicament of the Anthropocene or the *Capitalocene* as Braidotti (2019) puts it. The Anthropocene is commonly understood as a recent geological period associated with the detrimental impact of human activities on the planet. Humans' impacts on ecosystems have been attributed to massive and unscrupulous extractions of natural resources and exploitation in a profit-oriented and largely unregulated market economy. Despite more than 20 years of tourism research on sustainable development, Sharpley (2020) laments that very little progress has been achieved in this field. This failure is not only due to the entrenchment of neoliberal capitalism in many societies (Monbiot, 2016), but it is also caused by the vested interest of a few mighty villains (Weaver, 2011). Braidotti (2019) joins this conversation and adds that this neoliberal system of exploitation 'rests on advanced technologies, the financialization of the economy and the overwhelming power of the media and cultural sectors' (p. 40). Pertaining to the cultural sectors, educational systems (including researchers) are also impregnated with the values of the market economy. This explains why academic institutions embedded within this neoliberal system have been resisting change and maintaining the status quo (Dredge, 2022). The rise of conservative politics in Western 'democracies', blatantly revealed during the recent COVID-19 crisis (Bryce, 2023), has gradually been eroding the capacity of millions of people who aspire to live a simple, happy life, free from the fear of an authoritarian future. This remark sadly resonates with the observation made by Kumm and Pate (2023):

> As we survey our contemporary moment, as well as our own feelings and emotions, we are dismayed at the relentless diminishing of people's powers of existence. In the United States, we witness the sad affects in the banning of books, speech, and ideas - especially those that propagate the truth of racial, sexual, gender, and class injustice. We also see the removal of rights to bodily autonomy, privacy, and health care. Environmental protections are eroding; wages are suppressed; markets are manipulated; workers are exploited. We see widespread and open dissemination of lies and propaganda leveraged for political control. Mirroring global conflicts and struggles, sadness is all around. (p. 5)

Such an observation of the current situation intimates a rather gloomy, dire and even dystopian future. While this observation may be paralysing and distressing, it can also stimulate us to invent our own freedom. As Matteucci, Koens, Calvi, and Moretti (2022) argue, 'an affirmative philosophy of life appears more fruitful than indulging in denial and negativity' (p. 7). This was the stance of Albert Camus. Despite his rather dark view of the modern world as one of 'private and public techniques of annihilation' (p. 308), Camus (1951) refused resignation and was instead an advocate of individual and collective acts of resistance as the only way towards a possible 'renaissance' (p. 310). This is where, we believe, creative tourism, as a space of creativity, social connections, knowledge production and joy, may play a central role in resisting the destructive forces of neoliberal global capitalism. An affirmative philosophy entails political activism by overthrowing negativity through transformative collective actions that necessitate non-linear thinking and ethical praxis (Braidotti, 2019). A new materialist philosophy is affirmative in that humans and non-human subjects are intertwined, interdependent, therefore equally agentic, which calls for sensuous explorations of multiple assemblages of subjects, objects and transversal forces. As Deleuze would have possibly said, a more ethical exploration of tourism would require accounting for *local intensities*. Through this affective process, no one and nothing is excluded. This way of thinking is akin to the precepts of regenerative tourism (Dredge, 2022), which calls for 'developing conversational intelligence and deep listening' as alternative ways of knowing (p. 277).

Why do we see the creative tourist experience as a space of resistance with emancipatory powers? Firstly, the essence and the value of the creative tourist experience stem from relational encounters with people, practices, places, heritage and with a plethora of other non-human elements. Secondly, the affirmative philosophy underpinning the creative tourist experience opens the door towards more egalitarian relationships between tourists and hosts who both need each other to thrive in their respective communities. Thirdly, in creative tourist spaces, people get to feel the world more acutely; people learn, exchange ideas and experiences; people collaborate, get inspired and expand their own networks. Such relational encounters, therefore, are prone to foster local knowledge production (Braidotti, 2019), promote creativity (Bryden & Gezelius, 2017), care and preservation of heritage as well as stewardship (Duxbury & Bakas, 2021; Sterling, 2020). Furthermore, as White (2017) argues, relational encounters are critical to foment 'a socially inclusive political vision', which would produce relational goods (p. 133). By relational goods, we understand mutual respect, responsibility for others and ecosystems, altruism and, more generally speaking, social relationships imbued with an ethics of reciprocal care. Fourthly, drawing from Sacco, Ghirardi, Tartari, & Trimarchi (2019), we see the creative tourist as heterotopia, which functions as a sociocultural exchange 'platform of civic empowerment and capability building, in the context of a fairer allocation of power and control of resources' within co-constitutive heritage experiences (p. 206). Creative tourist spaces are, therefore, pockets of resistance (Matteucci, Koens et al., 2022) or machines of joy (Kumm & Pate, 2023) within mainstream tourism spaces of mass cultural consumption.

The creative tourist space is a site of actions, practices and performances; it is a space of experimentation; it stands for a bold rejection of inertia. This way, the creative tourist experience is a manifestation of empowerment, of making one's own freedom. While it may be a personal eudaimonic pursuit, through collaboration, openness to difference and an ethics of reciprocal care, the value of the creative tourist experience transcends the self to contribute to the well-being of the wider community. Rather than eudaimonia as individual well-being or human flourishing, the power of creative tourism lies in its production of collective well-being or what Onfray (2008) refers to as *social eudaimonia*. In our view, as Matteucci, Nawijn, and von Zumbusch (2022) argue, 'social eudaimonia can only be attained through resistance in the form of dialogical and creative social processes' (p. 177). This view is reflected in the idea of regenerative tourism, which entails developing 'an art to hosting good conversations, to nurturing the space for exchange, learning and transformation' (Dredge, 2022, p. 277). Although referring to social science inquiry, Fullagar (2017) sees in (new) materialist thinking a way to 'create generative and generous intellectual cultures that enable us to think rhizomatically as we negotiate the changing power relations of austerity, audit culture, marketisation of education and the rise of conservative global politics' (p. 255). Although the literature already provides a hint of evidence in this direction, we see in creative tourism the capacity to reclaim control over our lives, our freedom and over the prospect of a good life.

References

Agrawal, G., & Pato de Carvalho, C. (2021). Interview with Geetika Agrawal about vacation with an artist. In N. Duxbury, S. Albino, & C. Pato de Carvalho (Eds.), *Creative tourism: Activating cultural resources and engaging creative travellers* (pp. 68–72). Wallingford: CAB International.

Bell, C. (2015). Tourists infiltrating authentic domestic space at Balinese home cooking schools. *Tourist Studies, 15*(1), 86–100. doi:10.1177/1468797614550958

Bizas, E. (2014). *Learning Senegalese Sabar: Dancers and embodiment in New York and Dakar*. London: Berghahn Books.

Braidotti, R. (2019). A theoretical framework for the critical posthumanities. *Theory, Culture & Society, 36*(6), 31–61. doi:10.1177/0263276418771486

Bryce, D. (2023, May 16). When the world shut down around us: Travel restrictions and impact on family life during the Covid years. *Tourism's Horizon*. Retrieved from https://tourismshorizon938.substack.com/p/when-the-world-shut-down-around-us-d60?utm_source=%2Fsearch%2FBryce&utm_medium=reader2

Bryden, J., & Gezelius, S. J. (2017). Innovation as if people mattered: The ethics of innovation for sustainable development. *Innovation and Development, 7*(1), 101–118. doi:10.1080/2157930X.2017.1281208

Camus, A. (1951). *L'homme révolté*. Paris: Éditions Gallimard.

Camus, A. (1982). *The rebel* (A. Bower, Trans.). New York, NY: Penguin Modern Classics. (Original work published 1951.)

Deleuze, G. (1988). L'abécédaire de Gilles Deleuze. R comme résistance. *Interview with Claire Parnet*. Paris: Films du Losange. Retrieved from https://www.youtube.com/watch?v=voRRg3HBQnE

Deleuze, G. (1990). *Pourparlers*. Paris: Les Éditions de Minuit.

Dredge, D. (2022). Regenerative tourism: Transforming mindsets, systems and practices. *Journal of Tourism Futures, 8*(3), 269–281. doi:10.1108/JTF-01-2022-0015

Duxbury, N., & Bakas, F. E. (2021). Creative tourism: A humanistic paradigm in practice. In M. Della Lucia & E. Giudici (Eds.), *Humanistic management and sustainable tourism: Human, social and environmental challenges* (pp. 111–131). London: Routledge.

Duxbury, N., Bakas, F. E., Vinagre de Castro, T., & Silva, S. (2021). Creative tourism development models towards sustainable and regenerative tourism. *Sustainability, 13*(1), 2. doi:10.3390/su13010002

Duxbury, N., Pato de Carvalho, C., & Albino, S. (2021). An introduction to creative tourism development: Articulating local culture and travel. In N. Duxbury, S. Albino, & C. Pato de Carvalho (Eds.), *Creative tourism: Activating cultural resources and engaging creative travellers* (pp. 1–11). Wallingford: CAB International.

Duxbury, N., & Richards, G. (2019). Towards a research agenda for creative tourism: Developments, diversity, and dynamics. In N. Duxbury & G. Richard (Eds.), *A research agenda for creative tourism* (pp. 1–14). Cheltenham: Edward Elgar Publishing.

Filep, S., & Matteucci, X. (2020). Love in tourist motivation and satisfaction. *Journal of Hospitality and Tourism Research*, *44*(6), 1026–1034. doi:0.1177/1096348020927072

Florida, R. (2002). *The rise of the creative class and how it's transforming work, leisure, community and everyday life*. New York, NY: Basic Books.

Foucault, M. (1986). Of other spaces. *Diacritics*, *16*(1), 22–27.

Fullagar, S. (2017). Post-qualitative inquiry and the new materialist turn: Implications for sport, health and physical culture research. *Qualitative Research in Sport, Exercise and Health*, *9*(2), 247–257. doi:10.1080/2159676X.2016.1273896

Korstanje, M., Echarri-Chavez, M., Cisneros-Mustelier, L., & George, B. P. (2016). Creative tourism: Paradoxes and promises in the struggles to find creativity in tourism. *Journal of Tourism*, *17*(2), 41–52.

Kumm, B. E., & Pate, J. A. (2023). 'This machine kills fascists': Music, joy, resistance. *Leisure Studies*, *45*(5), 451–474. doi:10.1080/02614367.2023.2191982

Lenz Taguchi, H. (2012). A diffractive and Deleuzian approach to analysing interview data. *Feminist Theory*, *13*(3), 265–281. doi:10.1177/1464700112456001

Malinin, L. H. (2019). How radical is embodied creativity? Implications of 4 E approaches for creativity research and teaching. *Frontiers in Psychology*, *10*, 1–12. doi:10.3389/fpsyg.2019.02372

Massumi, B. (1995). The autonomy of affect. *Cultural Critique*, *31*, 83–109. doi:10.2307/1354446

Matteucci, X. (2013). Experiencing flamenco: An examination of a spiritual journey. In S. Filep & P. Pearce (Eds.), *Tourist experience and fulfilment: Insights from positive psychology* (pp. 110–126). London: Routledge.

Matteucci, X. (2018). Flamenco, tourists' experiences, and the meaningful life. In M. Uysal, J. Sirgy, & S. Kruger (Eds.), *Managing quality of life in tourism and hospitality* (pp. 10–23). Wallingford, UK: CABI.

Matteucci, X., & Filep, S. (2017). Eudaimonic tourist experiences: The case of flamenco. *Leisure Studies*, *36*(1), 39–52. doi:10.1080/02614367.2015.1085590

Matteucci, X., & Gnoth, J. (2017). Elaborating on grounded theory in tourism research. *Annals of Tourism Research*, *65*, 49–59. doi:10.1016/j.annals.2017.05.003

Matteucci, X., Koens, K., Calvi, L., & Moretti, S. (2022). Envisioning the futures of cultural tourism. *Futures*, *142*, 103013. doi:10.1016/j.futures.2022.103013

Matteucci, X., Nawijn, J., & von Zumbusch, J. (2022). A new materialist governance paradigm for tourism destinations. *Journal of Sustainable Tourism*, *30*(1), 169–184. doi:10.1080/09669582.2021.1924180

McCartney, P. (2020). Yogascapes, embodiment and imagined spiritual tourism. In C. Palmer & H. Andrews (Eds.), *Tourism and embodiment* (pp. 86–106). Abingdon: Routledge.

Menet, J. (2020). *Entangled mobilities in the transnational salsa circuit: The Esperanto of the body, gender and ethnicity*. London: Routledge.

Monbiot, G. (2016). Neoliberalism – The ideology at the root of all our problems. *The Guardian*. https://www.theguardian.com/books/2016/apr/15/neoliberalism-ideology-problem-george-monbiot

Onfray, M. (2007). *Théorie du voyage. Poétique de la géographie*. Paris: Grasset.

Onfray, M. (2008). *L'eudémonisme social. Contre-histoire de la philosophie V*. Paris: Grasset.

Pearce, P., Filep, S., & Ross, G. (2011). *Tourists, tourism and the good life*. London: Routledge.

Prince, S. (2017). Dwelling in the tourist landscape: Embodiment and everyday life among the craft-artists of Bornholm. *Tourist Studies*, *18*(1), 63–82. doi:10.1177/1468797617710598

Richard, V., Glaveanu, V., & Aubertin, P. (2022). The embodied journey of an idea: An exploration of movement creativity in circus arts. *Journal of Creative Behavior*, *57*(2), 221–236. doi:10.1002/jocb.571

Richards, G. (2016). The challenge of creative tourism. *Ethnologies, 38*(1–2), 31–45. doi:10.7202/1041585ar

Sacco, P. L., Ghirardi, S., Tartari, M., & Trimarchi, M. (2019). Two versions of hetero-topia: The role of art practices in participative urban renewal processes. *Cities, 89*, 199–208. doi:10.1016/j.cities.2019.02.013

Scherf, K. (2021). Creative tourism in smaller communities: Collaboration and cultural representation. In K. Scherf (Ed.), *Creative tourism in smaller communities: Place, culture and local representation* (pp. 1–26). Calgary: University of Calgary Press.

Sharpley, R. (2020). Tourism, sustainable development and the theoretical divide: 20 Years on. *Journal of Sustainable Tourism, 28*(11), 1932–1946. doi:10.1080/09669582.2020. 1779732

Sterling, C. (2020). Critical heritage and the posthumanities: Problems and prospects. *International Journal of Heritage Studies, 26*(11), 1029–1046. doi:10.1080/13527258. 2020.1715464

St-Pierre, E. A., Jackson, A. Y., & Mazzei, L. A. (2016). New empiricisms and new mate-rialisms: Conditions for new inquiry. *Cultural Studies – Critical Methodologies, 16*(2), 99–110. doi:10.1177/1532708616638694

Törnqvist, M. (2018). Rethinking intimacy: Semi-anonymous spaces and transitory attachments in Argentine tango dancing. *Current Sociology, 66*(3), 356–372. doi:10.1177/0011392116681385

Urbain, J.-D. (2007). Le touriste: Du sujet symptôme à l'homme qui rêve. *Synergies Pays Riverains de la Baltique, 4*, 15–25.

Waterman, A. S. (1993). Two conceptions of happiness: Contrasts of personal expres-siveness (eudaimonia) and hedonic enjoyment. *Journal of Personality and Social Psychology, 64*, 678–691.

Weaver, D. (2011). Can sustainable tourism survive climate change? *Journal of Sustainable Tourism, 19*(1), 5–15. doi:10.1080/09669582.2010.536242

White, S. C. (2017). Relational wellbeing: Re-centring the politics of happiness, policy and the self. *Policy & Politics, 45*(2), 121–136. doi:10.1332/030557317X14866576265970

Windress, K. (2016). Musical pilgrimages to Cuba: Negotiating tourism and musical learn-ing in Cuban Batá drumming. *MUSICultures, 43*(1), 132–152. Retrieved from https://journals.lib.unb.ca/index.php/MC/article/view/25263

Index

Printed in the USA
CPSIA information can be obtained
at www.ICGtesting.com
JSHW050043231124
74143JS00004B/84